ANTONIA SWINSON is a critically acclaimed writer and award-winning business journalist. After graduating from the University of Edinburgh she enjoyed a successful early career on Fleet Street, and for three years was TV critic on the *Daily Express*. Antonia moved with her family back to Edinburgh in the mid-1990s and for six years wrote a popular business column for *Scotland on Sunday*. She began writing about her allotment in 2001 for *New Consumer* magazine, and her 'Allotment Tales' have been appearing in *The Scotsman* since 2004. A former Chair of the Society of Authors in Scotland, Antonia is the author of three novels and one book on business ethics, the highly influential *Root of All Evil?*.

Also by Antonia Swinson

Fiction

The Widow's Tale (Gracewing, 1995)
The Cousins' Tale (Hodder & Stoughton, 1999)
The Love Child (Hodder & Stoughton, 2000)

Non-Fiction

Root of All Evil? How to Make Spiritual Values Count
(St Andrew Press, 2003)

Extended introduction to new edition of Arthur Swinson's
Scotch on the Rocks: The True Story Behind Whisky Galore
(Luath Press, 2005)

www.antoniaswinson.co.uk

YOU ARE
WHAT YOU GROW

Life, Land and the Pursuit of Happiness

ANTONIA SWINSON

with illustrations by Bob Dewar

Luath Press Limited

EDINBURGH

www.luath.co.uk

First published 2006

ISBN (10): 1-905222-64-5
ISBN (13): 978-1-9-0522264-3

The paper used for this book is FSC-certified and totally chorine-free.
FSC (the Forest Stewardship Council) is an international organisation
to promote responsible management of the world's forests.

Printed and bound by
Cromwell Press, Trowbridge

Typeset in 10.5pt Sabon

TO ALAN, RORY AND ELLA

My bundle of sticks that can't be broken

ACKNOWLEDGEMENTS

I would like to thank both *New Consumer* magazine and *The Scotsman* for giving me the opportunity to write about my allotment – and so much else besides.

Also my fellow plotholders at Saughton Mains allotments who have given me such a wealth of good advice, kindness and inspiration. Finally, I would like to thank my family, both for their forbearance and the unalloyed appreciation of the food I have grown.

CONTENTS

Ella, aged 11, at the Allotment (Illustration by Sally J. Collins)

INTRODUCTION

THIS IS A BOOK ABOUT GROWING. Not only food, but ourselves. In a stressed-out age, we are a pretty neglected lot, and
though this book shares a lot of trial and error and some good
gardening advice, it is most of all about nurturing ourselves
and understanding how the world works.

In a world of instant experts, I must come clean, for I am
no expert gardener but a writer who, thanks to an allotment
in central Edinburgh, is used to doing lots of thinking. The
plot that I rent for just £35 per annum from the city council
measures 60 feet by 30 feet. But as any allotmenteer will tell
you, an allotment is not just a bit of loam but the best bargain
on the planet. An allotment is not just ground for growing
food, but for growing ideas and new thoughts. So while spin
and disinformation carry on elsewhere, seeping through every
other part of our lives, allotments are the nation's secret power-
houses of creativity.

But you may ask, why should allotments be so special in
this way, compared to conventional gardens. Of course, gardens
are a fabulous haven for many of us, but in today's harsh
financial realities, there is a big difference. For unlike gardens
which today almost invariably come with a mortgage attached
(or 'bond until death', to give its actual meaning), allotments
come into people's lives unhinged from debt; a very deliberate
statement of intent. They are space in a stressed-out world
where we can think about the big questions normally tucked
safely behind the glued-down wallpaper of our lives. You go
out into the garden, but *to* your allotment; ground which is
part of a community, but also precious space in which to nurture ourselves.

I began working on my allotment back in 2001 with
my daughter Ella who was then nine years old. I had been a

financial journalist since the late eighties, and for a while I had been feeling that I needed to carve some space away from the web and the word processor and the shiny information world. Let me describe how the allotment looked on that first cold and windy April day when we arrived. An old barbed wire fence divided the plot because it had been redrawn by the council. There was a sunken swamp of couch grass and old wood where box beds had once been and what looked like a dying bush lurked in one corner by some straggly faded rhubarb. We opened the sheds and found a stinking mass of clothes inside.

Back then we did not stop to think about the previous occupant, an unknown gardener who had passed on to us what was to become a hugely important part of our lives. We knew nothing at all about him, apart from the fact that he had died the previous year from a long illness and his widow had decided she couldn't keep up the plot. We didn't even know his name. Yet what was evident, in spite of all the mess, was how much he had loved his allotment. I could see this in the terrace flags he had laid down, in the care with which the sheds had originally been built, even though the roof now leaked. And from the huge amount of stuff he had left – evidence of days and days of his life spent there, where he had eaten, shaved and lived. This ground had been his life. And now it was mine and Ella's. Yet why would this non-descript bit of loam in this crowded corner of south-west Edinburgh be such a thrill? Perhaps the penny had begun to drop: we are what we grow.

Shortly afterwards, I began writing about my allotment, first in *New Consumer* as 'Two Sheds Swinson' and then for *The Scotsman*'s Saturday Magazine, just for the sheer fun of it. It was a wonderful contrast to the vagaries of the stockmarkets, yet I found it was exciting re-interpreting the world through the prism of the allotment. Time has gone on and as the word count has mounted, I have found that these columns have formed a fascinating narrative; vivid snapshots of allotment life. Gardening writing yes, but not as we know it. I am delighted that thanks to Luath Press, these writings have been given a new lease of life.

I make no apology for writing about some pretty controversial issues facing us in the UK today. Making connections is my stock in trade, and I have come to realise that whenever we are prevented from doing so, others profit at our expense. When I began working on this book, my first task was to decide how to order the writing, describing as it does several years of allotment life experience. After a lot of thought, I have divided the chapters into seasons, rather than following strict chronology. This has the strength of bringing to life the allotment year, but it does mean that events and elements, such as my daughter Ella's age, are not sequential. Please bear with me on this. Each piece of writing is a snapshot of allotment life, and I hope that any inconsistencies will create an interesting basis of comparision.

As you will also see, by far the biggest section is titled 'Winter'. But then I do live in Scotland, which has long, long winters. I wondered at first what to do about this, and then I had a thought. Perhaps the great 18th-century Edinburgh Enlightenment came about as much due to those long dark days, as the departure of the Parliament to London? For if bright people could not sow seed or plough the land, they could always gather in taverns and think big ideas instead. So in putting together this short book, why should the humble 21st-century allotment not be a similar capital of the mind?

Allotments are land. But because they are often scraps of land rented by ordinary working people, they have never been taken seriously. I hope this book will help change such a perception. I believe that the time has come in the UK when we should stop thinking in self-limiting terms of gardens and gardening and start expressing our thoughts and feelings instead about land – our connections to it and how it defines us. Time to think about land and land issues in a new way.

Today, in spite of living in a world of apparent choice, we live in more prescriptive times. However much the Internet unlocks connections, we lack both time and peace to connect them up. Whom does that suit if we fail to connect? Not us. Life is short and not always lived to the most nurturing effect. If we are too busy to get earth on our hands, we become suspicious of mud. Yet... we are what we grow. So dig in!

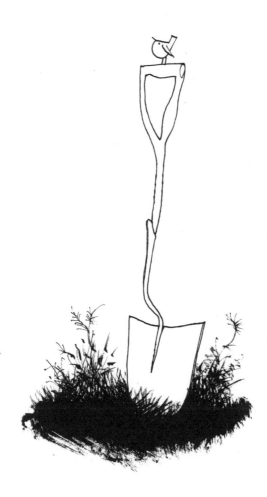

THE BEGINNING

First Take Your Plot...

'What! You? An allotment!' Howls of derision greeted this news in wine bars all over town. Astonished fellow journalists lifted noses out of Chilean red with the headline already forming. Carrot-top Shocker! Redhead Grows Green Fingers! Now if I'm honest, this disbelief is well founded; previous gardening experience consisting of navigating my path from front door to taxi without crushing the dandelions, and one interview conducted years ago for the *Sunday Express* which took place in the Kensington garden of a famous designer. Halfway through, she suddenly screamed at me to get my hands off her saxifrage; I told her I'd never even met her husband.

Hence the idea of me digging for victory is surprising, but my friends should know better. It began with money but as a financial journalist, I have come to learn that the best adventures usually do.

In the case of my allotment, money came into it over months of me exclaiming 'how much?!' in disbelief in supermarkets and farmers' markets while standing at the organic fruit and veg. The price premium met my customer resistance. And yet, like everyone else, the GM food debate and ongoing diet of stories of chemicals spewed onto our food sickened me. So I would hover empty-handed in front of the veg counters, talking to myself.

Matters became even more complicated when I discovered it was not a case of organic (good, wholesome supporting small farmers) versus GM (wicked, unhealthy spawn of bastard global corporations). A scientist friend – the one I'd always phone if ever on *Who Wants to be a Millionaire* – informed me that the label 'organic' can mean pretty much

anything in some countries. A nice dosing in raw sewage
would qualify. So finally, determined to find a new way of
eating where I was in control, I rang my local council's
Parks Department.

There is a myth that allotments almost disappeared post-
Second World War. This is just a property developer's pipe
dream. Google 'allotments' and 24,700 pages pop up.
They're everywhere and getting more and more popular.
The food scares in the nineties started the comeback, but the
emotional uncertainty following September 11th sent
enquiries soaring. So, if you live in Warrington you have 16
sites to chose from, while down in Hampshire, Winchester
offers 20 acres of prime downland with plots costing just
£20 a year. Visit the website of the National Society of
Allotment and Leisure Gardeners for the latest allotment
news for England and Wales (www.nsalg.org.uk) and north
of the border, try the Scottish Allotment Gardeners
Association (www.sags.org.uk). Unlike other hobbies
such as, say, salsa dancing or weaving classes, the sense of
ownership, adventure and wonderment you discover is a bit
like becoming a first time parent. Wow! Feeling responsible
for another living thing – only this one, thank God, does not
demand 2am feeds or a second mortgage in childcare.

Appropriately, I was on the waiting list exactly nine months,
during which I made regular solicitous calls to my new man
– the City Allotment Manager – and I now bore colleagues
and strangers at bus stops with bad photographs. Do you
know, mine has two sheds, one bench, a small terrace and
60 by 30 feet of black loam...?

I've had my allotment a whole month and unexpectedly find
myself rather popular. Friends discover you can drink
Chilean red sitting on a bench just as easily as in the local

wine bar and light up without anyone giving you dirty looks. OK we're still surrounded by weeds (have you seen what passes for male talent near me?) but here where we sit is south facing, overlooks a river, and my garlic and onions look rather good. Two months ago I'd have told you Brassicas was a wine bar franchise, but now I know better. My brand new *Veg Grower's Guide* tells me you have to rotate this crop: just what I've been saying for years to girlfriends, who never stop moaning about the turnips they live with. Best of all my new paradise is just five minutes' drive away. OK, I know this is just a bit Not Green, but you try walking 20 minutes in these heels.

WINTER

Most people define themselves by their work and family. In which case, I have been a journalist and writer for 20 years: TV critic for the *Daily Express*, feature and business writer for the *Daily* and *Sunday Express*, business columnist for *Scotland on Sunday* and author of five books. I am also lucky to be the mother of two smart, fun children and have stayed married to the same rather extraordinary man for two decades.

But let us return to the title of this book and look at our lives in terms of what we have grown in the course of our lives. It might cheer us up at a barren time of year when we must remind ourselves we are still gardeners... and that if we are lucky, life is full of seasons.

So what have I grown? My first garden, from birth to 18, belonged to a sprawling Regency house just five minutes' walk from St Albans Cathedral, where we grew raspberries, rhubarb, mint and many flowers. We had a lawn just about big enough to act as a badminton court, so my brother, sister and I would smash up the peonies most summers as we honed our backhands. There was also a Victoria plum tree which contained a tree house where I would lie for hours eating the crop and reading – Puffin books at primary school, and then when I discovered boys, steamy teenage romances like the 'Angelique' series, for which I would do battle at local jumble sales with the formidable nuns from the nearby Sopwell nunnery.

My father Arthur Swinson was a successful author, playwright and military historian, whose own gardening forte was hollyhocks, raspberries and blackberries. A lovely man, he overworked and died aged just 55 when I was 13, leaving to his name over 30 books and 300 plays.

It was during the winter after his death when I first had an

inkling that I could make things grow. Some years earlier I
had visited the Jersey estate of his rich brother and his wife. It
was there I saw the Jersey cabbages; huge boles on giant stalks
which were used for producing walking sticks. The housekeeper
had given me a few seeds and for some reason it was only now
that I planted them. Extraordinarily, I managed to grow one in
the back garden and wrote about it in a letter to *The Times*.
The letters editor, perhaps thinking it made a nice change
from non-stop letters about strikes and power cuts, actually
printed it. The local *Herts Advertiser* sent a photographer and
I still have the picture of me standing next to that ten-foot
cabbage. No one in the home counties had ever seen one before.
I received letters from all over the world, including one from
an Australian farmer who thought it would save a fortune in
animal feed.

After my father's death, life spiralled downhill – my brother
went off to boarding school, my sister left for university and
my beloved grandmother died. I poured myself into school
work and singing lessons, and while others sampled Queen
and Motown, I planned to be the next Callas. At weekends, I
worked as a waitress in a tea garden to earn money to go up
to London each week to the English National Opera. Tourists
sat at tables amongst the flowers eating cream teas. These
days of course, bereaved teenagers like me would be in grief
counselling before one could say probate, but those were the
last days of Empire-building grit and the British stiff upper lip.
Like many people with unresolved grief, I stopped growing
and stopped looking. Certainly nothing growing in that tea
garden registered, because nothing had any colour. At 18 I
failed to get into the Guildhall School of Music and Drama;
they said I had a beautiful voice but when I sang, nothing
touched my eyes.

Thankfully, a gap year in Rome started the cure. Here

were formal dusty gardens with olive trees, iron chairs, parched bourgainvilleas and palm trees. I would walk on my way to work through the formal gardens at the Villa Borghese eating ice cream, watching the fierce blue sky towering above the city. The following year I moved to grey, windy Edinburgh and into university life. One summer's day, I took a bus to the Royal Highland Show at Ingliston near Edinburgh's airport. The sun was shining, and for the first time I noticed Scottish gardens: how neat and tidy they were, how full, how profuse in roses. Gorgeous roses, spilling over and whipped by the wind.

After graduation I moved to Glasgow – where the constant rain spreads weeds and seeds in all directions – before finally arriving in London. First stop Notting Hill, where home was a poky flat in Blenheim Crescent. Newly-weds, Alan and I christened it Hardboard Hall, thrilled to find it came with a key to a communal garden filled with rhododendrons. At the annual summer garden party, bankers and their wives mingled uneasily with the shabby bohemians, who had bought in before the riots. We would saunter down Kensington Park Road into Holland Park where squawking peacocks would fly up into the trees.

I suppose everyone is entitled to a misspent youth. I worked as an actress in a soap, in London's West End and in TV comedy and radio drama. I performed in Glasgow panto, sang for knives and forks and was a professional voiceover, pounding Soho's Wardour and Berwick Streets armed with a repertoire of voices. I taught English as a foreign language in South Kensington to assorted warring Iraqis and Iranians and developed an enduring love of Lebanese food. I also worked in my stepfather's small film company, and then began to write, and since then I have never stopped.

The next season brought a baby and a move to the other side of the Shepherd's Bush roundabout to Chiswick, first the

Acton end and then the pretty hemmed-in bit by the river. For the first time ever, I owned a garden of my own. As anyone who knows London gardens will tell you, they are precious, every inch of them, because of the crush of humanity which surrounds them and the roar of tubes, and buses, and trains. In Chiswick, we heard Concorde's twice daily supersonic boom. How we lowly vassals would look up in wonder at its haughty aristocratic profile. While we always grumbled about the Heathrow flight path, somehow we never questioned Concorde's *droit de seigneur* over West London's air space.

My first Chiswick garden had a Russian vine from hell, a huge ceanothus and a pear tree, which every two years covered the lawn in fruit. Each morning, I would take my baby son Rory out for a few minutes' bonding time, pointing out the flowers and the butterflies, before guiltily handing him over to his nanny. Chiswick garden number two was smaller, prettier, with a rowan tree and lots of bulbs; a party garden. At this time I became a trustee of Chiswick House Friends and learned a new gardening language, with words like *patte d'oie* and ha-ha. Then in 1995 came the big move to Scotland. It was August, and we enjoyed several leaving parties in London gardens. Everyone said we would be back, no question – no one could live without London. They quoted that well-known Dr Johnson line that being tired of London means being tired of life, but we arrived undeterred in the middle of what everyone said was the hottest summer Scotland had enjoyed for years. I wore my Loden coat and felt chilled to the marrow.

North Berwick is a salty little town on the Firth of Forth, where the wind cuts through teeth and hair and plants. People become accommodating Uriah Heeps, bent ever so 'umble against the wind. I found myself desperately missing family and friends and those little London gardens. How could I ever emulate the neat Scots who planted in such firm, effective rows?

Or earth myself in such a feudal society where everyone knew their place? I learned quickly that here, land has a very different connotation in a country where so few own so much. I opted out. No more gardening for me in the conventional sense. And so began my life in pots. Soon I had dozens of them, painted in bright colours. I found they went with the grain of my low boredom threshold, because when I grew bored I could move them about. *The Times* gardening correspondent wrote up my Scottish roof garden, where both a vine and a camellia contrived successfully to survive the Scottish winters.

The last season to date has been the move back to Edinburgh. Like 'Doc' in *Back to the Future*, I keep expecting to meet my younger student self coming round the corner. And on my allotment, without being conscious of what I am doing, over the last five years I have planted a summation of my life: black hollyhocks, raspberries and a plum tree remind me of child-hood; roses reconnect me to those vivid early student days in Edinburgh; while sweet potatoes reminisce of being young and happy in shabby long gone Notting Hill. The camellia from that North Berwick roof terrace astonishingly still lives on, offering 20 or 30 blooms a year. A straggly pear tree – bought more in hope than expectation from Woolworths – provides a faint memory of fumbling motherhood, of a green eyed baby boy, who, now 19, strides across my life at a height of six-foot-two. I have even reclaimed that gap year in Italy, planting yellow broom – *la ginestra* in Italian, the subject of Giacomo Leopardi's finest poem – and a bald persistent little vine which clings to life by the shed door.

So my allotment is a map which plots my life and shows that I am what I grow. *Most* of the allotment I should say, for of course Ella has her own patch and her own future, and must make her own way in the world...

NOVEMBER

Dig in for a Special Sort of Urban Living

I am no seasoned gardener but an 'allotmenteer', which involves a very different sort of gardening. Think mud and pioneering spirit. Think very old clothes and very good food. No phone, no e-mail and no one to tell you that there are mud streaks down your face and twigs in your hair. Allotments: in a stressed-out world, everyone should have one.

Forget the old stereotype of ferrets and flat caps, for allotments nowadays teem with people of all ages and nationalities keen to grow organic food: from students and green-fingered families to pensioners and groups of friends sharing plots for fun. When my daughter and I collected the keys three years ago, we faced not only an overgrown plot full of couch grass and mares' tails, but also our own ignorance. Yet we were given advice, and found a rare kindliness and sense of community. This is a very special sort of urban living.

At weekends, the winter allotment is alive with the sound of hammering, as allotmenteers weatherproof sheds and cold frames before getting stuck in to the weekly bonfire. Then comes the real joy of sharing tales of triumphs and disasters over hot chocolate. My top crops this year were rhubarb, mange tout and onions, but the carrots flatly refused to germinate and my Caribbean sweet potatoes were a knobbly joke.

However, this week I am making fertiliser by soaking comfrey and nettle leaves in rainwater; and planting garlic, which loves cold weather and is great for home cooking and giving as presents. Just separate into cloves and push down into holes around six to eight inches apart and cover thickly with mulch – the colder the weather, the thicker the layer. On an allotment, seasons become sharply distinctive. Early winter brings a feeling of peace as experienced allotmenteers call a truce with the birds and leave berries and seedheads for food. Perhaps I'm too much of a soft touch, for I've been adopted by a gang of crows who appear to consider flying south for the winter to be for sissies, and yell 'cor!' at me from a nearby tree.

Despite the cold, there is still much to pick: tasty leeks and Brussels sprouts, which miraculously, my kids actually eat without me resorting to bribery; celery for soup; brambles; and – best of all – fat, juicy Autumn Bliss raspberries. The canes now lean drunkenly in the wind, but are still laden with fruit. There's just not quite enough to take home so, naturally, with the morning sun on my face, I have to polish them off there and then. Tough job, but someone has to do it.

Lessons from my Father

In 1962, my late father, Arthur Swinson, spent weeks in the Western Isles researching the truth behind the story of the ss *Politician*, the *Whisky Galore!* ship, which ran aground in 1941 carrying 20,000 cases of malt whisky. Armed with his tape recorder, he obtained extraordinary interviews, and his book *Scotch on the Rocks*, a bestseller in its day, revealed a grittier and even more exciting tale than Compton Mackenzie's magical fiction. It was also remarkable travel writing, recording vivid first impressions of island life in the 1960s.

One day, after interviewing the widow of Charles McColl, the Customs officer famed for his dogged pursuit of the islanders and their whisky, Arthur stopped to congratulate a woman working in her garden. He had been struck that no one on Eriskay or the Uists cultivated their gardens. She was an incomer from the Lake District, who always planted daffodils and tulip bulbs each autumn because she missed spring gardens. Though as she explained, 'the blast' would come in from the sea so strongly that 'after a gale you go out into the garden and it looks as if there has been a fire, all the plants are black'. Walled-in gardens didn't help because the wind 'would get inside and spin like a top'. For Arthur this was extraordinary. He couldn't imagine life without a garden.

A few weeks ago, in his footsteps, my family and I spent a week's holiday in Lochboisdale. I visited the widow of the former headmaster on Eriskay, a remarkable lady whose splendid walled garden, sheltered by a hill, was green and thriving. In extraordinary counterpoint, there on her wall was a photograph of her husband leaning against the *St Joseph*, the island's only motor boat which Charles McColl had commandeered for his chase.

My father had a professional plantsman in his background. His mother's father had been a gardener at the Deanery in St Albans, tending grounds near the cathedral which then stretched down into Roman Verulamium. (Devotees of Anglican realpolitik will know it is always the Dean not the Bishop who snaffles the best real estate in any cathedral town.) Raspberries were my father's particular talent. They were always bigger and tastier than any in our neighbourhood. I suppose that is why about a third of my allotment is devoted to them. Childhood memories sharply re-emerge as I work among the canes, the tang of fresh Autumn Bliss when eaten is an instantly comforting connection to a gentler time. And, of course, they also taste great soaked in malt whisky.

Rising from the Ashes

Christmas is coming, heaven help us. Everywhere shops are filled with santas and tinsel and crowds. Yet there seems to be a desperation this year in the celebrations, as if the UK economy needs to squeeze just a little more lifeblood out of the poor punters.

The effect of this on me is a yearning to be in a money-free zone where I can rest my eyes from the crowds, the garish lights and fake Christmas cheer. So I come down to the allotment with my daughter Ella. Though the ground is hard and dead, and there is little colour but for the yellow and blue paint of our sheds and fencing, we potter around, drinking hot chocolate from the thermos and planning next year's campaign like a pair of battle-hardened armchair generals.

In the spring, I plan to be organised earlier with raspberries, while Ella fancies a mulberry tree. In the shed I read to her a favourite Jacqueline Wilson story about a little girl with a mulberry tree. The story itself is depressing (contemporary children's fiction makes me want to slit my wrists half the time) but the

description of the mulberries is tempting. We are
optimistic. Our fig tree and kiwi fruit are now invisible
under layers of fleece. Our neighbours think we are mad,
given that our current cold weather front is coming straight
from the Siberian plains, but allotments are the stuff of
dreams and fairy stories. That is why they are so good for
the spirit, not least at this time of year, when the human
spirit is reduced to the status of a walking profit centre.

It is also good to take stock over the past year. Victories
are notched up: my Italian salad was fantastic and saved a
fortune at the supermarket, the potatoes were also delicious
and the onions too, which are now plaited artistically round
our kitchen. There was also the back-breaking reclamation
of the whole plot from couch grass, and lots of beetle-
covered wood. Next season we shall have a completely
cleared site. Yet the high points of the allotment year
have been as much about other people, as about plants.
In August, a TV gardening programme came to film myself
and Ella at the allotment. This was a great treat for Ella
and won her brownie points at school. The downside was
a week or two of people looking at me oddly in shops,
but it wore off. I don't know if I could ever enjoy losing
my anonymity. It is something we take for granted, but
it is also a form of wealth that celebrities don't enjoy.
This year we have also made many new friends; of all ages,
nationalities, ideas and backgrounds. In the allotment,
the world is our oyster.

Then there were the bad moments. The very worst happened
one Friday evening in June. Ella and I arrived as usual to
enjoy late-afternoon sunshine to find the larger shed had
been broken into. Vandals had trashed it, lighting a fire and
burning the floor through. The walls were black with soot,

my tools blackened. It was a miracle the curtains had not
caught fire, and the whole lot burned down. Chillingly, the
vandals had left the screwdriver which had forced the door
open, neatly upside down in the earth. I wish Ella had not
seen it all. For the very first time she was faced with mind-
less evil. Perhaps she was lucky to have reached ten before
encountering it. Bursting into tears, she called it the worst
day of her life.

Neighbouring plotholders rushed over. One lady brought a
towel and soap and washed Ella's hands and gave her a
cuddle. Others helped us clear out the burned debris – a
favourite rug I'd had since school which we used for picnics,
a wooden table, vegetable books – while other items were
unrecognisable. We called the police and two very polite
officers came round. Sympathetic as they were, they did
imply that painting the sheds yellow was asking for it: that
same line which somehow excuses rapists. They gave me a
crime reporting number and left. I discovered that other
sheds on the site had been broken into but none had been
burned out like mine. The next day we heard that the gang
had gone to three other allotments in the town. They had
been busy.

Somehow it galvanised Ella and I. Steel went into our soul.
We power-hosed the walls and repainted them. We bought
a lino offcut, repaired the floor, and washed the curtains.
A week later plotholders were visiting us and pronounced the
shed better than ever before. The incident brought out the
very best in human nature and we made even more friends.
Ella then asked if she could join the Allotment Committee to
discuss security! Committee members were amazed that a
ten year old wanted to join, and they agreed to let her speak
at the AGM. Ella planned her speech carefully and it was

delivered with a steely glint in her eye. This babe meant business. God help the vandals next time. I suppose it was meant as a compliment when someone said we had a young Maggie Thatcher in the making.

A Load of Rubbish Feeds a Fertile Imagination

Hurray! I received junk mail this morning. While most people snarl and bin it, I am always deeply thrilled when the financial services industry targets me in order to add to the UK's £1 trillion debt mountain. 'Can I have some more, sir?' say I, Oliver Twist-style. For quite apart from keeping the poor swine who write this usurious drivel in gainful employment, I'm in desperate need of it for my three compost bins, which stand, Dalek-like, at the corners of my plot. Junk mail keeps my compost from getting too moist, you see. And frankly, at this time of year I need all I can get.

Arriving at my allotment yesterday, I found that one bin had fallen over in the wind. No mean feat, as it was full.

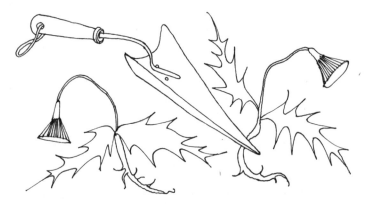

Lucky me. There, piling out, was thick, black, earthy humus which, having rotted down nicely over the last 18 months, represented the miraculous transformation of all my coffee grounds, teabags, vegetable peelings and shredded junk mail. I spread this lovely muck on one bed and felt hugely clever. Now, bin empty, all I have to do is start again.

As the average household produces around 200lb of kitchen waste a year, we gardeners have a great excuse to save land-fill. Compost improves soil structure, texture and fertility and stimulates healthy root development by providing food for microorganisms which, in turn, deliver the right balance of nitrogen, potassium and phosphorus. That's the science, but compost-making is also satisfyingly creative, perhaps most of all at this commercialised time of year, for it is a blow we can strike for self-sufficiency. The shop tills may be ringing, but no one is making a penny from us. Rather, it is we who are taking advantage. New credit card offer? Three pages? That'll do nicely.

I suspect that for many gardeners compost-making becomes a secret obsession, dictating our actions even when not gardening. Do I feed my family more stews because of the vegetable peelings they create? As for all those eggshells produced from baking, who'd say no to home-made cake? (Even mine.) Chores such as emptying the vacuum cleaner and gathering lint from the tumble dryer hold exciting significance. I have not quite reached the point of haunting hairdressers to request hair off the floor – being pleased to receive junk mail is madness enough – though on the bus last Monday I did count eight hair salons en route. Dare I go in with a carrier bag and a sweet smile? What do you think? All in a good cause. Can I have some more, sir?

Make the Shift to Thrift

It's déjà vu all over again. For years, writing a weekly business column for *Scotland on Sunday*, I would find myself cast as resident Cassandra, writing about the debt Armageddon the nation faced. Through the late 1990s and into the zeroes, despite other exciting stories – the Asian crisis, the Russian default, the Millennium bug, Enron, World Com – there it was: the UK's personal debt mountain.

By the time I wrote *Root of All Evil?*, a book on money and ethics, published in 2003, the debt mountain topped £850 billion. Surely, I thought, it can't go any higher. Wrong. According to a Debt Free Direct UK survey, we now top £1.1 trillion, with Scots the most prone to put off dealing with credit card bills until it's too late.

While there are good debt counselling services available to look at nitty gritty bills, it seems to me that we must deconstruct our hard wiring about money and consumption, to save our peace of mind, bank balance and, let's face it, what's left of the planet. We need to redefine needs, not wants, and work out how we can obtain them without parting with cash.

The connections between spending and feelings of self-worth and anxiety are well known. Allotments banish anxiety and build both happiness and self-esteem to magical proportions. Perhaps the government should purchase land for allotments to stave off bankruptcies, and keep the economy ticking over, because they provide such good financial education. Spending on your plot, you see, is rather frowned upon; allotment culture remaining hearteningly imbued with wartime thrift.

So here are some allotment tips to start the process of bringing your consumption habits down to earth:

- Cut yoghurt cartons up into 'sticks' instead of buying high margin plastic labels.

- A large, old table fork bought at a car boot sale makes a wonderful weeder.

- Save seeds now to save you buying them.

- Salt is a cheap weed killer; and bulk-buy bran does for slugs.

- Never throw out a bit of wood. Someone on your site could use it, and it will build social capital, more valuable than financial capital to a factor of four.

- Grow perpetual spinach for a never-ending supply of cheap salads/great soup.

- Use half plastic bottles as cloches for young plants. No, you don't buy expensive bottles of fizzy drinks: ask other people for theirs, and let them pay the dentist bills.

Say it with Flowers

This may sound unlikely, but I do believe that at this fevered and expensive time of year, allotments hold the secret of a happy, non-dysfunctional Christmas. Ah-aah, you may say, anyone can escape the madding crowds, skulking away in the shed with just BBQ sausages and hot chocolate for company. And you would be right. But whether you believe we are celebrating the birth of Jesus or a mid-winter pagan binge, allotments are the secret of happy families, providing both a sense of control and a bit of mystery too.

Firstly, with some advance planning, allotments have great potential for present giving, particularly if you have children. And my goodness, how much high moral ground there is to be dug! The baby boomer generation, so sociologists tell us, has apparently reached the top of its 'hierarchy of needs' (in ordinary speech this means they don't need to fill their houses with any more 'stuff'). What this have-it-all generation value now are services, experiences and gifts imbued with what is called 'social capital'. This basically means something that is indicative of that non-financial wealth which comes from a sense of community; something we all need to survive during a time of single living and fragmented family life. Increasingly, it's the thought that now counts more than the designer label.

And so, in such a social climate, allotments come into their own. Freshly grown garlic with the stalks painted gold and prettily presented are a hit, as are onions picked in September, arranged into long plaits and given perhaps a blue French beret. Dried lavender can be sewn into bags for drawers and wardrobes to repel moths, or else lavender flowers can be picked in autumn while fresh and made into lavender water. Winter flowering shrubs – my forsythia always bursts into life just before Christmas – make marvellous wrapping decorations instead of ribbons or fancy stickers. For an added soupcon of capitalist postmodern irony, I have been known to use copies of the *Financial Times* for wrapping paper! For keen cooks, bouquets of mixed herbs are always welcome; mint leaves can be presented in a fancy wooden box for tea; or frozen gooseberries picked in July can be defrosted to make fresh crumbles. Or how about herb bread, made with grated rosemary or sage?

Cheapskate, moi? Certainly not. In the age of the New Consumer we must re-think how we consume and how we give. Why should we be shy of giving something of ourselves at Christmas? And is it such a bad message to teach children that they should first think how they can make something they need themselves, before they start whining for the money to buy it?

As for receiving gifts, how often do we look at our presents by 26 December and think, what a sad collection? How much Christmas cheer is founded on the commercial exploitation of both giver and producer? Goods, too often made in sweatshop conditions, are flown thousands of miles to the West for the Christmas market, to be marked up and paid for with debt, still being serviced by Easter. 'Lucky' recipients then write letters of false gratitude, thanking people for presents that they either recycle for someone else not to like, or use petrol taking them round to the charity shop. What an enormous amount of wasted money, energy and world resources.

At least since acquiring my allotment I can ask specifically for things I need and want. And where the mystery comes in, is that every allotment is unique. From most friends I ask for cuttings, which I grow in pots and plant out in the spring. But for others I also cultivate each year a special Christmas present wish-list to suit every pocket. Here are five of the best:

- For the ultimate in posh bulbs: the Heritage Bulb Club
  Spring collection (www.heritagebulbs.com). Based at
  Tullynally Castle in Southern Ireland, the club sends out
  monthly, rare bulbs with full historical information on
  their part in world art and literature. A recent example
  was their pink cyclamen coum, which has marvellous
  dark green leaves and red flowers. The plant notes
  revealed that the cyclamen root was used in a medieval
  treatment against hair loss and assisting in childbirth.
  By the 17th century however, it had graduated to being
  thought handy as an aphrodisiac when crushed.

- Cheaper and really practical for compost gathering,
  is the Clean-up Canvas made by Allsops
  (www.harrodhorticultural.com) – the ultimate Mexican
  burrito, only this one has handles and is designed to take
  the hassle out of clearing up autumn leaves.

- Cheaper still, but extremely useful is the 'Man' Tool
  Cleaner from the Organic Gardening Catalogue
  (www.organiccatalogue.com). This scraper, handmade in
  Forestry Stewardship Council certified oak, dates back
  to the days when navvies dug the canals. It was said
  that clean tools made the difference of an extra man in
  the piecegang. Allotmenteering certainly can bring on
  navvying tendencies, but clean tools do last longer and
  make gardening easier.

- Hence why, with a clear conscience, all outstanding
  Christmas money can go towards a Jekyll Weeding Fork,
  designed by the head gardener of garden designer
  Gertrude Jekyll, available from Hortus Ornamenti
  (www.hortus-ornamenti.co.uk). Don't leave this behind
  in your shed, it's too special. Great for keeping dande-
  lions/in-laws/kids in order.

- For spring, offer your nearest and dearest the chance to be thought of every time you enter the allotment. Exclusive to Thompson & Morgan (www.thompson-morgan.com) is the Blue Lagoon Verbena. Fragrant deep blue flowers make a marvellous splash of colour in clumps edging the allotment.

The Nation's Silent Storytellers

At this time of year allotmenteers can only dream of future pleasure. Yes, I have ordered my sweet potatoes and onion sets. But the ground is covered in frost and however much I look at the colour photographs in the catalogues, it is hard to imagine that my allotment will be anything other than a rock hard, no-go zone for weeks.

So I am devoting this column to looking not forward, but

back. To the past. Asking, just what are allotments for and
why are they here? It is important to understand that
whether or not we ourselves have an allotment, they remain
a vital link to our common history, to the land from which
our forebears – unless rich and titled – were cleared long ago.

The first allotments in the UK were found in Lands End in
Cornwall, originating from roughly 100BC and still in use
today. Strip farming by peasants was the norm in Saxon
England, but between the 10th and 16th centuries land was
gradually carved up between the descendants of the Norman
conquerors and the Church. The commoners were pushed
out into ever smaller bits of commonland, tied to the land
and the lord body and soul, in bonded servitude.

Then came the Dissolution of the monasteries which, as land
was confiscated, led to ever greater aristocratic landholdings.
After which, enter stage left, Elizabeth I. These days we are
used to seeing flattering TV programmes about her, conditioned
into thinking that for England she was a class act. But for most
of our ancestors, she was anything but good news. Under her
reign, 'enclosures' – the closing off of common land from the
people into the landowners' domains – intensified.

The very word 'enclosures' emphasises the fencing off.
I prefer, however, to call these forced dispossessions the
'English Clearances'. Sadly, because they happened at a time
when few ordinary people could read and write and, unlike
the Scots, the English lacked the clan system and an oral
storytelling culture, there was little means outside folk songs
to pass on the data of what happened from one generation
to the next. And although the awful cruelty of the English
Clearances is in our DNA, when explaining our national
attachment to our gardens, our consciousness of the truth has
disappeared, very conveniently for some.

In the 17th and 18th centuries, the enclosure of peasants' common land increased. The Diggers – brave non-conformist men and women who fought the landowners' hegemony – held out in places like St George's Hill Weybridge, now home to pop stars and diplomats (see *The World Turned Upside Down* by Christopher Hill). However, the enclosures of common land continued. People moved into towns, becoming fodder for the Industrial Revolution. But by the late 18th and early 19th centuries there was increasing concern among the intelligentsia about the poor nutrition and overcrowding in the towns, leading to model villages and small areas of land being set aside for commoners. There was growing fear too of a French-style revolution. So in 1845 the General Enclosure Act empowered the commissioners of enclosures to provide the first allotments as we know them today.

Yet such was the footdragging by landed vested interests that by 1870, out of 615,000 acres available, only 2,200 acres (0.3 per cent) had been set aside for plots. So in 1887 came the first Allotment Act, forcing local authorities to provide allotments if there was demand. Of course local authorities, controlled by local business interests, were hardly keen. So in 1907 the Smallholding and Allotments Act imposed responsibilities on parish, urban district and borough councils.

The First World War saw allotment activity increase, but pressure for housing in the 1920s and 30s saw sites disappear. By World War II there was so little allotment land available to 'Dig For Victory', that public parks had to be dug up to grow food. From the 1950s to the 1990s, when the organic food movement began across the UK, developers won legion battles for allotment land. For example, in

Edinburgh in 1906 there were 105 allotment sites; today there are fewer than 25.

Allotments must therefore be considered a microcosm of our own history. They were set up out of the landgrabbing Establishment's fear of revolution, a sop to replace the land our forebears lost. Yet as Kevin Cahill details in his book *Who Owns Britain*, the effects of successive land grabs remain with us to this day. Our struggles to pay the mortgage and coping with a lousy worklife balance, is all as the result of UK property prices being predicated on an artificial land supply. 99.9 per cent of us are still squashed onto 7.5 per cent of the UK land mass, while less than 0.1 per cent of the population (just 189,000) own or control 70 per cent of the land.

How often do we visit National Trust properties, marvelling at the parterre grounds, little connecting what hunger and injustice our ancestors suffered to create them? And disconnection with our history seems complete, when the radical Henry Doubleday Research Association sees no irony at all in putting Prince Charles on its latest magazine cover. For however genuine his interest in organic food, he is one of Britain's most acquisitive land owners, a living embodiment of why in the UK, we must work so hard and live in such debt to keep a roof over our heads.

The time has surely come to renegotiate our relationship with the land. Next time you pass by allotments, pay a silent tribute to the men and women who kept them going. For allotments are not just ground for growing food, they remain the nation's silent storykeepers, telling us where we came from, and how very much has been taken from us.

DECEMBER

A Little Dig at Justice

The phone rings. It is the police to say they have finally caught the vandals who trashed my shed and plot. As they have confessed to dozens of other crimes in gardens (necessitating huge amounts of police paperwork, by the way) they are going to court. If I want to, I can write to the sheriff asking for restorative justice.

My mind goes blank, before I remember that this means practical reparation: in this case, digging allotments. I congratulate the PC on his colleagues' success, and say that I think restorative justice for these young men is a great idea, though not anywhere near me. Nothing can ever repair the horrible feeling of discovering your hard work ruined, of looking around and taking in the calculated malice. Suddenly, I picture the latest mid-evening, reality gardening show. Three spiky-haired, deeply cool teenagers repay their debt to society, while digging for TV stardom. With the high turnover of TV formats, it is surely only a matter of time.

In spite of the vandals' attentions I can report one happy ending: our freezer is filled with fruit and vegetables for Christmas dinner, so I can bore my family from the position of well-tended, high moral ground. Brussels sprouts; small, tasty French beans; broccoli florets; and top-and-tailed gooseberries for creamy puddings for those who hate Christmas pudding. The trick is to freeze fast to keep the flavour. Another triumph is long plaits of onions hanging around the back door, ready for roasting whole. I particularly like the Long Red Florence variety from Italy, which is torpedo-shaped and full of flavour.

As Christmas approaches, the peace and space on an allotment, the absence of advertising and crowds of crazed shoppers, can be extraordinarily restful. So whenever the sun shines I come down to the allotment with my daughter Ella.

In the spring I plan to be organised earlier with parsnips, which I love, while Ella fancies blueberries. We are nothing if not optimistic. Allotments are the stuff of dreams and imagination. Anything is possible, which is why they are so good for the human spirit.

A Good Time to Dig Deep

How I value my allotment in the run-up to Christmas as a priceless breathing space from crowds and consumption. The more tender plants are now trussed up in white fleece, like small Miss Havishams, but there's always pruning and composting to complete – as well as reading seed catalogues in the shed while drinking hot chocolate out of a Thermos flask. Try it!

Allotmenteering definitely shifts entrenched views – and not least about Christmas. Why all this shopping hysteria when it is obvious we already have far too much 'stuff'? At my local car boot sale, expensive items, often unopened, are flogged for less than five quid. So let us consider other sorts of giving.

Charity Aid Foundation vouchers are a brilliant idea (www.allaboutgiving.org). Send vouchers of £10 or £25 to friends to donate to a favourite charity – no wrapping, no postage, only good feelings. But in 2005, Make Poverty History year, I am going one further, and asking friends and family to donate the cash value of our reciprocal presents to one worthy cause which is all about allotmenteering – Ghana-style.

Gift Amu Logotse is a Fife-based lecturer and performing artist who, a few years ago, while on a home visit to his native village of Wumenu, had the bright idea of approaching the tribal chief and asking for a patch of waste-land for an experiment: self-help cultivation for unemployed youngsters. Involving the whole community, he built a water tank and ploughed the barren land. The first growing season was so successful that the chief gave more land. Three years on, the Wumenu Community Farm employs 30 people and produces food for the whole village. This is not some top-down, emotionally manipulative, celebrity-drivelling UK charity, but a local, flexible community project which goes with the grain of tribal and family loyalties. Amu now raises money for the farm through his increasingly popular school visits across Scotland.

Think what we spend on the average UK Christmas present, or at our local garden centre, then consider what effect that same money would have in Wumenu. A palm, mango or coconut tree seedling costs £1.50 in local money; a flock of hens and a shelter or three goats and pen is around £50, while housing for four families in the African modular style costs just £250. Donors are kept fully informed and are invited to visit.

Hold earth in your hands and you instantly feel bonded to other nurturers of the soil, whichever sky they live beneath. Time to connect, perhaps.

Keep Going, Keep Growing

Somehow I never quite adjust to our Scottish winters. Absurdly, they always seem to spring on me unexpectedly. It's the cold that throws me: the marrow chill which only lentil soup and whisky seem to touch. And those winter feelings of deprivation: the lack of sunlight, the leaving and returning home in the dark, and not seeing garden plants and herbs for a week at a time.

And then separation from the allotment is an ache. When I do manage to get down there, often it is only to dump household waste in the compost bins, pick some leeks and flee. In this extreme cold there is no pottering about, weeding or blethering with friends.

No. I cannot not grow anything until next March. So I consider sizing up the office windowsill for a herb garden. Yet I have a feeling that both colleagues and the office cleaners would be unamused. Who would water them over the holidays, and who would be such a saddo to come into the office to feed my plants?

Perhaps someone should invent a screensaver which consists of a slowly growing plant requiring virtual watering, and which dies if I leave it untended. Perhaps someone has, and there is a kind reader out there who could send me the details? For allotmenteering is not just a frame of mind but a

private obsession, which spills right out into the rest of one's life. I could be at a conference, wearing my suit, and a fellow delegate only has to mention this column and how they grow food too and it's very hard not to talk carrots instead of strategy.

Hope is at hand, however, thanks to the Organic Gardening Catalogue (www.organiccatalogue.com), which has provided many happy journeys to work. They obviously know their customers' predilections, for 2006's catalogue has a particularly good section on winter growing. So if you have a cold frame or sheltered pots, you can grow Vitamin C-laden greens and keep your sanity. My Claytonia, otherwise known as Winter Purslane, is already sprouting well despite the Mongolian winds, and the Louviere Corn Salad is a real trouper with good frost resistance.

There is also Winter Cress, rich in vitamins and minerals, which I am growing in pots outside my back door. So as I hurry out or into the house in the cold winter days, I snatch a handful and, as I munch, remind myself that allotmenteers are just like actors between jobs. We are just 'resting', that's all.

You Are What You Grow

Dr Gillian McKeith is putting the fear of God into every home in Britain. Have you ever looked at that table display of a week's fatty processed food at the start of *You Are What You Eat* and thought, that looks familiar? My daughter Ella, 13, is a keen convert to McKeith's gospel. No more tea in the morning; we must drink hot water with lemon. No more crisps; just nuts and sunflower seeds. We also check our tongues for cracks with remarkable enthusiasm. The show coincided with taking on our allotment, and both of us have seen our interest in nutrition soar. However, this month, thanks partly to my desperation to keep gardening through the winter, we have graduated to a higher plane and begun sprouting seeds.

Sprouting seeds are cheap, tasty and the most nutritious of

foods. It's all to do with unlocked enzymes, which are
woefully deficient in our processed, overcooked diet.

One could live on sprouting seeds and nothing else, so high
is their nutritional value. In his book *Survival into the 21st
Century*, Viktoras Kulvinskas says that if we had to live in
an underground shelter and could take only one type of
food, the top choice would be alfalfa seed, with fresh water.
They apparently bring big improvements to digestion, energy
levels, moods, libido and immunity to illness.

No longer does Swinson mooch around health food shops
feeling inadequate. These days I grow mung beans with the
best of them. So if La McKeith stomped into our house, and
said 'aduki', we would not say 'bless you', or stare blankly
at the camera, we could say it is good for kidneys. We also
have chickpeas, alfalfa and fenugreek. Soak on Saturday and
Tuesday for sprouting Sunday and Wednesday. It's easy, just
a matter of getting organised and squashing the notion that
you must wear open-toed sandals all day. Sprouting seeds
are also fantastic timesavers for lunchboxes. They don't need
washing, taste sweet and work as snacks or in sandwiches.

The Organic Gardening Catalogue
(www.organiccatalogue.com) offers a Sprouting Seeds Starter
Pack, which includes 'The Sprouter's Handbook' and alfalfa,
chickpeas, red clover and broccoli seed, which is reputed to
stimulate the body's defence against cancer. So I'm bringing
my allotment home this winter and looking after my family's
health at this rather fragile time of year.

Here's Mud in Your Eye

There are times in life when, unfortunately, you are forced
to clean up your act. Literally, in my case. Nine months on

from getting the keys to my allotment and I have
rediscovered my childhood tomboy tendencies, happiest in
muddy gumboots and hopelessly unfit at weekends for
polite society. Yet if you are invited out to a meal in a top
restaurant on Saturday night, as I was recently, polite society
decrees you simply must NOT arrive with mud-encrusted
nails, bits of twig in your hair and dubious smudges on your
cheek. It is also not respectable to have more clothes in your
wardrobe with knee patches and rips, than designer labels
and shoes, which leave half the mud in the county trailing
behind you. Alas, this was the challenge I faced after a day
spent pottering around my two sheds (painting inside for a
laugh and so in my hair, yellow paint had stuck to the
twigs). Last Saturday night my destination was Edinburgh's
newest, chicest restaurant, the Forth Floor in our brand new
Harvey Nichols.

It took about an hour and the best part of a loofah, plus a
pithy contretemps with a husband who flatly refused to let
me take a string of home-grown onions for our friends over
one shoulder, but eventually I was scrubbed and dressed up
to a passable level. And if the highly professional waiters did
notice the odd bit of paint under the designer lights, they
were much too polite to comment.

I was enjoying my second cocktail and stunning views of
the Castle, when I suddenly realised that as the allotment
takes up so much spare time and money, I had barely eaten
for leisure in a restaurant all year. Yet what a difference
in the experience. Back in my old London life, when
I would pop into 'Harvey Nicks', for some posh nosh, frankly
I was hyper, so busy talking I never tasted the food. Yet now,
months of home-grown produce had apparently re-educated
my taste buds, encouraging me to take time to savour the

seafood starter and (oh, what sweet revenge) some delicious
rabbit pie.

A memory of my old London life also surfaced that evening.
For years I would take the train to Waterloo to work and
just before it crossed the bridge at Chiswick, I would see the
allotments and idly wonder what sort of sad person could
waste so much time with them. I suddenly saw myself back
then – designer suit, designer briefcase, designer ideas and a
child who hardly saw me. Who was the sad one then?

With an allotment too, seasons begin to mean something.
Frankly, a life spent working in an office and slumping in
front of the telly causes seasons and weather to merge together.
But now, each season is special and distinctive. Winter on
the allotment brings a feeling of peace. Experienced
allotmenteers call a truce with the birds and leave berries
and seed heads for food. Perhaps this first year I've tried
too hard, for I have been adopted by a family of crows who
seem to consider flying south for the winter is for sissies,
preferring to 'cor, cor, cor' at me from the riverbank.
There are also goodies still on offer: Brussel sprouts,
spinach, salsify and corn salad. My own winter favourite,
which makes great Christmas presents, is fresh garlic.
My Italian friend Giuseppe, who works three plots along,
is famous for his, which he uses in his restaurant. My own
specimens alas, are distinctly weedy. I made the mistake of
buying a packet of three at the local supermarket and
shoving in the cloves. Not, I now learn, a good idea; you
should buy proper garlic for planting. Cheap shortcuts do
occasionally work though. I bought a bag of organic tatties
from the local supermarket back in April, having missed the
seed potatoes in the garden centre, and they were stunningly
successful.

Real joy is sharing our year's triumphs and disasters. OK, so my carrots and parsley flatly refused to germinate, but the onions and squashes did me proud. As we swap these tales, there is no keeping up with the Jones, instead everyone has a fierce interest in each other's knowledge and a desire for us all to succeed. This leads to genuine creativity, which the management consultants I write about tell me is 'innovative synergy', now sought by all successful companies these days. Amazing: we manage to achieve this without expensive management consultants (or dodgy accountants) assisting us.

For the weekly bonfire in winter, Giuseppe uses thick yellow fat from his restaurant kitchen which he brings in big buckets. How I envy him with that huge blazing fire. The smoke smells of rosemary and I dream hungrily of chicken 'alla romana'. No weed is safe. However, as colourful Italian phrases rise up with the smoke, I secretly wonder whether he is actually venting feelings about his stressed-out designer customers, who are too busy talking to taste the food.

JANUARY

Help Your Child Grow

Contrary to myth, children are welcome on allotments, particularly if they are keen to learn and lend a hand. My daughter Ella was nine when she began her allotmenteering career. I thought she would run a mile, but instead she relished the challenge. Now freshly painted inside and out, Ella's shed has an old table, a chair and even bunches of hanging dried flowers. Who needs computer games when a girl has her own real estate?

Children and allotments. I can imagine your horror. Yet even toddlers and allotments can work well with a bit of preparation, and the advantages for family life are far greater than just fresh veg. For example, it doesn't hurt children to learn about boundaries while still young: not walking on other people's plots, or screaming. They see their parents regularly in a new environment, happy and unstressed, while time out in the fresh air does wonders for a child's mental health.

Allotments also teach children social skills, for here they can interact safely within parental earshot with strangers of all ages, backgrounds and nationalities. Older allotmenteers are often born teachers, and can be a real blessing for children whose own grandparents live far away. Allotments are traffic free, providing endless opportunities to see wildlife. At various times of the year our own regular visitors include herons, wrens, crows and a large fox.

This month, Ella and I have been mulching in barrow-loads of manure. From the beginning, I gave her responsibility for her own mini-plot, so now she is keen to work with me.

At home, a pop-up mini-greenhouse is invaluable for getting seedlings started early, making the allotment part of daily life, whether she can visit it or not. A wooden indoor plant house is on her birthday list.

As many schools find, there is nothing like growing produce to give children a huge interest in preparing and eating good food. Radishes, mustard and cress are quick and tasty, while curly kale is delicious eaten in handfuls. Ella is also the proud owner of a large gooseberry bush, which has inspired her to learn to cook proper old-fashioned fruit crumble. She looks at me in awe when I tell her that when I was her age, I used to have it for school lunch most days, with extra custard on Fridays.

Grassroots Democracy

A cutting from the *Daily Bruin* arrives by post from an American student friend. No, this is not some cartoon invention, but the student newspaper of UCLA (University of California, Los Angeles). It is a beautifully written piece about LA's South Central Community Garden and its 350 plotholders' titanic struggle for survival against the bulldozers. If you earn your living from politics, local government, community development or the law, or are involved in popular campaigning, do visit their website (www.southcentralfarmers.com). Their story has much to teach us. And taking place in California, nothing is done by halves.

In 1992 after the LA riots, 14 acres of the city's industrial no-man's-land was donated to a city food bank which then lent it to locals to cultivate. Shut up in housing projects far

from parks or fresh food, these are the immigrant invisibles
who make up the city's vital army of janitors, maids and
warehousemen, drawn from all over Latin America. Over the
years, at their own expense, they have created an extraordinary allotment garden of 360 plots. They grow produce too
expensive to buy in LA supermarkets: cherimoya, Inca fruit
normally seen in the Andean foothills of Peru, papaya,
figs, aloes and gourds, and rare herbs sought by local
doctors such as pipicha and huaje. The article vividly
describes family life on the plot, handmade hammocks
slung between guava trees and folding chairs set under
avocado trees. It is an oasis among factories, storage units
and warehouses, a world away from Beverly Hills. One
Mexican plotholder describes it as a sanctuary, 'a hunger of
memory... a place you have when you want to come back to
a time when you felt good about your life'. How many UK
allotmenteers could say the same?

Villain of the piece is property developer Ralph Horowitz,
who was originally forced to sell the land to the city, but has
now successfully sued the city, forcing Los Angeles to sell it
back to him for $5m (£2.8m). He is quoted as saying the
families will be thrown off the land by the sheriff. Yet locals
are now mounting an extraordinary campaign, perhaps only
possible in this Internet age. If you have a free moment this
weekend, why not think global and e-mail your support to
Antonio Villaraigosa, the increasingly defensive LA mayor?
For at the story's heart lies a moral argument, quite distinct
from legal realities, one which has shaped our own history,
dictated our ancestors' lives and bequeathed us our sense of
displacement. Who really 'owns' the land? The weak who
love it and cultivate it, or the strong with the big money,
plans and political connections who can kick them off?
Why should history ever only be a one way bet?

Deep in Muck and Music

This is one of the best stories I have ever covered as a business journalist. One which showed that music can be created in the strangest places, transcending even rigid laws of market economics, because of its power to tap into the fathomless potential of the human spirit.

One day the phone rang. Did I know that a Glasgow forklift truck company had just appointed for six months... a composer in residence? A what? A top of the economic cycle story if ever I heard one, I thought cynically.
Still, Christmas was fast approaching and, under pressure to fill my business column with something less yawn-making than Gordon Brown, I hotfooted it down to Glasgow. There, amid the oily workshops, a young composer with a growing reputation was working with staff in their lunch hour making music... with instruments made from bits and pieces of forklift trucks. An amazing sound, Bauhaus style, very gritty, 1930s Germany. Well, I thought, certainly a whole new meaning to Vorsprung Durch Technik. The fact that both she and most of the staff told me they had allotments and tried out new musical ideas in their sheds only added to the air of unreality. Any moment I expected Sir John Harvey-Jones to arrive with a TV crew, in a business version of *Surprise! Surprise!*.

Months later, I was invited back for the staff performance at the firm's anniversary party. The latest forklift truck models were on display and the workroom teemed with clients. Extraordinarily, unlocking staff creativity through music making had doubled productivity and sales were booming. (All the publicity hadn't exactly hurt either.) Management schools are missing a trick here, I thought. The staff's performance was breathtaking and I could see all the business-men in suits in the audience were itching to have a go. I've never looked at forklift trucks in B&Q the same way since.

Most of us do not have such enlightened employers, but our allotments can work miracles for music making. In a crowded noisy world, they create mental as well as physical space for our creativity to thrive, whether we feel like gardening or not. Somehow being covered in mud, feeling free, really does bring out that inner child. Don't worry about the noise bothering the neighbours, they're as chilled out as we are.

Children always lead the way in allotment music making, exploring the syncopation of sticks banging tin drums or plant pots, or seeds swishing inside tubes. Older children fill jars with different water levels from the hose, and play tunes sitting high up on shed roofs. Why is making your own music in the open air seriously magical? On the web the other day, I came across Yorkshire installation artists, whose unique selling proposition to galleries is making work from bits and pieces picked up from allotments. A brave new world of profitable artistic self-expression perhaps, but not surprising.

Allotments are also the best places to listen to music. Really listen to the notes, rather than the half-listening we normally achieve in the car or kitchen. Working with the earth and plants somehow provides the right level of concentration, or absence of distraction. Hence why most plotholders work with headphones or have a radio hanging precariously from the fence, with gardening styles often reflecting our musical taste.

The Radio 3 and Classic FM brigade go in for lots of flowers in clumps. So while the rest of us at this time of year are working on plots of mud, they already have their nice clumps

of crocuses and early daffs poking through. Jazz babies like
me who like Fitzgerald and Holiday are enthusiastic diggers
and levellers of the ground, rarely happy until mud has
reached the knees. Give me the earthy blues or gritty
modern bands at this time of year when planting 'Andover'
parsnip seeds. My favourite new CD belongs to a new
discovery, Marlevar, an exciting Italian folk group, who tour
with the Chieftains and sing in Italian and Provencal, with
an edgy Arab twist. Check out their website
(www.cdroots.com/hr-marlevar.html).

Of course, for the more uninhibited, there can be silent
karaoke sessions too. Once her own plot is nice and tidy,
my young daughter enjoys standing on a log, earphones of
her Sony Walkman plastered over her ears, strutting her
stuff. I can always tell when it's Beyoncé's *Crazy in Love* by
the fast wiggles!

Having a range of ages on the allotment also means we can
look forward to plenty of Andy Stewart, Perry Como, Roger
Whittaker and er, Shirley Bassey. Did I mention how one's
'cool' disappears? A certain business journalist was observed
belting out a Bassey-esque chorus of 'Green Finger' last
week, while taming garlic in the cold frame. (Da-dadada-
dah! He's the man, the man with the path weed spray! etc.)
Yes, there goes the markets.

And it gets worse. Opera. This
month, grown men planting broad
beans in loo rolls, as brother
Titchmarsh advises, are
disturbingly prone to that opening
number in Mozart's Marriage of
Figaro, and 'Vin-chair-roooooo!', a

well known football anthem allegedly written by songwriting duo Pavarotti & Turandot. How lucky we are to have a Sicilian family on the plot to keep us right with the words! Note for future reference: humming theme tune to *The Godfather* – NOT a good idea.

Keep Going, Keep Growing

I always enjoy receiving readers' letters, never more so than when they challenge and surprise. I was therefore delighted when a resident of Edinburgh's New Town informed me that this column had been the subject of hot debate at the New Year meeting of his local residents' association.

My correspondent enquired whether allotments should not be kept for the 'seriously poor', and means tested to keep out the burgeoning army of middle class kitchen gardeners. If not, then allotments should surely be charged out at existing land rents, reflecting, particularly in Edinburgh and its environs, high land values. The city's annual allotment rental was, he felt, clearly absurd.

Given that historically, allotments were a pragmatic sop from the landed establishment to the starving, urban poor, dragging allotments into the market economy is certainly a revolutionary idea. Yet my reader has a point. Italian friends, recently visiting from Le Marche, explained to me that similar plots there would cost around £35,000. This doubtless explains why Scotland's Italian community, even at this less than sunny time of year, value their *ortaggi* so highly.

I was mulling over this letter on my plot, snapping off the juicy heads of Brussels sprouts stalks for soup, when I realised that my radical correspondent had just seized the new zeitgeist. For if even allotments are up for debate about how much they could raise for council budgets – a sure sign of a re-rating – so increasing numbers of well-informed, highly taxed and debt-burdened people are asking just how much do landowners contribute to the common good? Not least the 350 families who own more than half of Scotland's private land, much of which is registered offshore. Unsurprisingly, the old political argument about land value taxation – originally promoted by the New Town big daddy of free market economics himself, Adam Smith – is now being discussed seriously in political circles north and south of the border, not least among the Chancellor's officials. The idea being that, as in Denmark or Australia, the rental value of land should be taxed annually for local amenities, given that it is community economic activity, not land owners, which creates the value of land.

Pre-First World War, the Lords defeated proposed legislation and years of war, depression and subsidy meant land has remained off-limits for fiscal discussion. Until now. Yet in our ever greener realpolitik, I suspect allotments will remain zero-rated, on peppercorn rents. Though I'm open to Italian-style negotiation should my local parks department ever wish to be paid in pepperoni.

Every Little Bean Counts

Last week at work I had the auditors in. No, not the usual sort. These were social auditors, skilled in assessing 'triple bottom lines': the social, environmental and economic impact of organisations. Daunting, yet just one week on I can see how it will save time, money and resources. Social auditing means counting outputs as an entity. For what is not counted and labelled is not accounted for and therefore doesn't exist. When the Florentines invented double-entry bookkeeping in the 13th century, God and *la famiglia* were a given, but in today's global marketplace we count selectively. Very convenient for those in control of the money, but less so for ordinary people.

On the Internet there is a fascinating social audit published, of 180 allotmenteers of all ages, and covering a range of urban, suburban and rural locations (www.idrc.ca/en/ ev-85414-201-1-DO_TOPIC.html). Interestingly, the research team identified that given how much smaller modern properties are becoming, the desire for allotments is on the increase. It suggested that councils need to make more provision for them in future.

As for that triple bottom line, economic benefits included saving money, the good effect on house prices nearby (if well kept) and cheap organic food. Environmental benefits were: green space, habitat for wildlife and buffer zones in urban areas. Social benefits were: friendship, exercise, fresh air, learning new skills and quality of life.

All good stuff. Yet in a world where decisions are too often justified in bald terms of economic impact, let's unpack the economic benefits of these supposedly soft social elements. What could the estimated financial bottom-line cost be to the NHS, council social services, and the Benefit Agency if the 180 plotholders on my site were not allotmenteering and therefore had poorer long-term physical and mental health? Hopelessly uncountable?

Well, let's say one small plot keeps one retired lady fit, active and happy and out of a residential home for just one year. Taking the current Scottish average for residential and nursing care of £39,000 per annum, suddenly her allotment acquires new value. So time perhaps for a political re-rating of allotments. Any generous social auditors out there up for some er, groundbreaking research?

Zen and the Art of Allotment Maintenance

I realise that the spirituality of allotments is not the usual subject for weekend gardening pages, but reading recently that GPs are being urged by the government to coax the nation off anti-depressants, it is maybe worth a line. For in a dissembling world, full of spin, stress, mis-selling, disinformation, and unrealistic targets, I believe it is the spiritual peace allotments provide that lies behind the joy allotmenteers so often feel.

Now readers may wonder why allotments could be more spiritually special than, say, ordinary gardens? Perhaps the reason is that plot-holders must travel to their allotments, and once there, can only stay for a short time. Maybe it is this commitment, combined with limitations of time and distance, which provides the mechanism for observing nature closely. With such intensity of concentration mental space develops for deeper thoughts, and with it, the right conditions for spiritual growth – as necessary for health as any vitamins. With practice, if one believes in God, we might even hope for a little two-way conversation, if He feels like getting in touch.

This does not mean of course that allotmenteers float around in some sort of holier-than-thou reverie. Trust me, our language gets distinctly fruity when couch grass roots refuse to yield, or slugs, foxes and vandals do their worst. Yet this is a parallel moral universe where good and evil engage in constant, honest battle, and all of life is here. This week, for example, I am planting parsnips, that most delicious and underrated of vegetables. Sliding over my trowel comes the longest worm I have ever seen. Just watching him ooze away into the black earth has an extraordinary therapeutic beauty, and the moment fixes itself into my mind's eye.

Unless one is retired, time for allotmenteering is short, slotted tightly between home and work. Hence the reason I opt for box beds – I can work half a bed in half an hour – I am also expert in keeping clean, so I can visit en route to the office. 'Just where is my spiritual space?' I sometimes ask myself as, clock-watching desperately, I belt back to the main road.

Yet allotments' secret alchemy works when it chooses. In the small hours, when, like millions, I find myself wide awake, work worries piling up in a mental in-tray, suddenly the allotment may come into my mind – the beauty of that solitary worm, the smell of the air, the promise of those neatly spaced parsnip seeds. I am instantly at peace. Love in action – who knows? For it passes all understanding and all logic too.

Plot for Citizens' Rights

Last week I attended a family funeral. Unusually, this was not a cremation but a burial, an expensive plot having been purchased from the local council.

As we stood at the freezing graveside, I couldn't help thinking that burial plots are somewhat like allotments in the sense that they are a very personal space in a very public arena. For just as we allotmenteers express ourselves and our creativity in our plots of public earth, so in a cemetery the names, dates and family ties of real people are displayed on gravestones for all to see.

And of course, in an overheated property market, cemeteries, just like allotments, occupy predominantly urban land and are inconvenient for those who would prefer the land to be used for development. How many burial plots and allotment sites over the years have been allowed to fall into disrepair, crocodile tears shed as money changed hands?

Cremations are much more convenient for the powers that be, because they mean that ordinary people don't take up space. Their equivalents in allotment terms are the increasingly popular potato 'towers' which flourish on UK balconies.

How extraordinary that we put up with our apparent lack of importance. A story from the Borders caught my eye before Christmas. Apparently cemetery space is fast running out and desperate councillors, while debating the building of a new crematorium, approached the Duke of Roxburghe to buy some land. Given how much local people do for his family, one might have thought an acre or two would have been a reasonable, and astute, gesture. The request was refused. Apparently his refusal has been accepted.

According to *Who Owns Britain* by Kevin Cahill the current duke owns 55,500 acres in Roxburghshire, with a further 10,100 acres in nearby Berwickshire – even more than his predecessor owned in 1872, when the Return on the Owners of Land revealed 51,459 acres and 9,959 acres respectively.

The question we and the Borders' 105,000 inhabitants might ask is this: just what are ordinary people worth? Are we merely units of economic activity, or do we have value beyond what we can earn and consume?

As for Borders Council, I have only two words to say apropos his Grace: compulsory purchase.

SPRING

DIGGING FOR CONNECTIONS

SPRING IS THE SEASON of hope and promise. Obviously. When the plants finally wake up and decide to start sprouting in all directions, how can it not be really exciting? Yet spring is a challenge not to be underestimated. There is always that moment in March when a cruel sun suddenly slices through the window, exposing all the dust and cobwebs. It is not a pretty sight. I suspect that is why suicide figures are always at their highest in March; the worst of the winter may have passed but if fixed points are not there, the idea of another spring can be unendurable because its promise cannot be fulfilled. So I tend to treat the season with as much caution as pleasure. We survivors need to be gentle on ourselves. For if we are what we grow, then we need just as much nurturing as our plants.

Perhaps it's time to ask *why* are we what we grow? Why is this attachment to our gardens and our allotments, to the very earth itself, so very strong? So very personal? Almost as if it is a huge part of some identity we only barely recognise? Why when we move house is the parting with the garden so much more traumatic than leaving behind the bricks and mortar? In spring we are supposed to spring forward, but if we

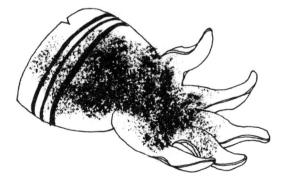

are to add up to ourselves perhaps it is a case of back to the future.

When you next fly over the UK, look out the window. Take in the patchwork shapes of the fields. What an empty country we live in, so different from the overcrowded island in our media's world view. This is where our ancestors grew their food, allotmenteers before the need for tiny allotments. They did this for centuries before the enclosures for livestock – the fencing off of common land to provide beef and lamb for the rising mercantile middle class. History is always a case of follow the money. Trouble is, for most of us, there is a disconnection with the land which feeds our sense of incompleteness.

Many of us have perhaps been inspired to trace our ancestry, by the BBC genealogy series *Who Do You Think You Are?* I have 'done' the lines of all four grandparents, finding myself a North and South mixture of Kent, Lancashire, Staffordshire and Herts. But the trouble is, tracing our ancestors' roots before they came into the towns too often means hitting a disconnection, a brick wall.

According to the 1871 census my great-great-grandmother was Jane Johnson who was born in Wales. But on the day of the census she was a single mother of three, living in the Liverpool lanes and earning her living as a charwoman, which I understand in those days meant cleaning out bakers' ovens. This was the sort of reality experienced by the vast majority of our ancestors. But she would not always have been so desperate. Whereabouts in Wales did Jane's family come from? Where was home? Family rumour says the Bangor area, and this is likely, given its proximity to Liverpool, but I have come to value paper evidence over family tablets of stone. Questions replace answers. Did Jane speak Welsh? Did she have a strong singing voice? What did her family care about most, how did they use money and what did they grow?

Few of us born in the UK can trace our ancestry back to 1066, and so most of us might as well be adopted for all the knowledge we can glean, once we have sifted through all the family disinformation and reinvention and hit the end of the census records. Where do we come from? Geneticists will tell us we can all be traced back to a few folk in Africa, but that is not the point. Where was the land where our ancestors settled? The brick wall remains, but knowledge and love of the land remains deep in our DNA. And when spring comes, we react to it just as our ancestors did.

Our unquenched thirst will explain why, in the UK, we haunt garden centres and spend a fortune on our gardens. We visit stately homes but do not consider the injustices suffered by ordinary people, whose dispossession allowed these estates to be created. Do we ever stop and think even for a second, just where the successors of those poor folk who once loved the land they tilled, now live today? Let alone reflect, as we shell out our money in the stately home gift shop and on entry to the special collections, that these losers could be us! Of course not. Yet we are still marked by this past and cannot escape it, however new our consumer durables may be. We just need to start reading our history in a new way.

So look out of that plane window. If you are flying into Gatwick you will see that fields near the area of population tend to be long and curved in shape. This is because early enclosures were fenced-off strips of land, which followed the line of the early strip farming, the line made by horse and plough. It was always pretty inefficient space wise, because every family had a strip and then a piece of land next to it for access. Once crop rotation was introduced, this system stood no chance. But people suffered all the same. And their suffering and hunger from being unable to feed their families must still be taken into the equation.

Enclosures pre-1750 were administered through local arrangements, and principally seen as a means of forcing masterless men off the land and into employment. Work as social control. Later enclosures in the 18th and 19th centuries bolstered by acts of Parliament, were much more neat and tidy, with communal obligations, privileges and rights declared void for all time. The system worked a treat – for the big land owners. Enclosures could only happen if the owners of four fifths of the land to be enclosed were in favour. So given that the local land owner could draw the map, there were in-built disadvantages for smallholders and local peasantry. The land was then available to be rented out at a commercial rate to tenant farmers and with a mature legal system designed to establish land title, so capitalism was born. It was Adam Smith who wisely pointed out land no longer produced merely food but rent – capital. As ordinary folk could not keep their families with what they grew, they had to work longer hours for other people. This provided the conditions for Britain's industrial revolution.

This brought about huge changes to society, and the mental construct which had been developed over millennia of communal land for common grazing was destroyed within just three hundred years. Aping his superiors, an Englishman's home became his castle and anything communal was seen as suspect and dodgy. Even today, allotments are decried as messy, an anomaly; even a minor threat to the natural order of private property.

Of course this is not entirely unchallenged, from the right-to-roam legalisation and the foxhunting debates to the booming popularity of allotments. There is continued re-examination of the Green Belt and interest in political circles, in the old Lloyd George cause of taxing annually the rental value of land for the community to pay for infrastructure. A new mood in a mature democracy. But we must also start to question old land ownership patterns, because history has so much to do with our present situation and why we have lost touch with where we come from.

As I have written earlier, Google the word 'enclosure' today and you will find fencing companies far further up the page than any account of the English history of dispossession. As least the Scots' term 'Clearances' pertains to people. However rich we may feel in our standard of living, we are the poor and dispossessed, because even if we would not be seen dead strip farming, our mortgages we slave to pay are actually debt vehicles created to supply housing on an artificially tight supply of land, artificially tight because of the enclosures. This is not at all an overcrowded island of the tabloid mantra, just look out of that plane window.

Our problem is the way history is presented. Historians prefer the viewpoint of the powerful, who gave titles and title deeds to each other. To be fair, the incontrovertible fact is that the rich leave a paper trail and the illiterate poor do not, but there is also a value judgement being made which does not serve the majority well. One which implies that ordinary people, badly dressed with bad breath, bad teeth and dirty faces could never be exciting, could never have ideas or ambitions. 'Rude mechanicals' as Shakespeare found, are best left for comedy.

However, what is less funny is how over the centuries we

have become, very conveniently, divorced not just from the ownership of land but just as potently, from any sense of communal or spiritual kinship. Trespassers Will Be Prosecuted. Private Property Keep Off seems to be our only written constitution. And as we have moved on from the 19th, 20th and now into the 21st century, whom has this suited? Divorced from the land, how much has consumerism – enriching others in the process – replaced deep down connections with meaningless plenty? How sad it seems too, that in such a prosperous age we are mortgaged and indebted, too bowed down to enjoy all the goodies, too busy working to parent our children, and all because of an artificially tight land supply.

In between the cracks in the story of land and land ownership, our very history has disappeared. Who are we, and where are we from? Most people move around for economic reasons and so reconnecting the land of our ancestors is pretty much a question of luck – something we need if we are going to find out more of our story.

I have mentioned Jane Johnson, my mystery great-great-granny from Wales, but in digging up the past, my own really lucky find was in the Swinson line. Here I have been able to reconnect to land in an area I had no prior knowledge of at all.

One spring day a couple of years ago, thanks to the Internet and the research efforts of an energetic cousin, I found myself standing in front of the cottage where my ancestors lived in the late 18th century just outside the North Staffordshire village of Oakamoor in the Churnet Valley. This rural corner of England had been a centre of iron production for seven hundred years, but by the late 18th century locally mined copper was king. Thomas Bolton & Sons produced highly sought after copper wire which by the mid-19th century provided the raw material for telegraph lines – the Victorian Internet. The Boltons were reasonably enlightened employers by the standards of the time and built their workers' cottages and a chapel. But on the Internet recently, I found a photograph of men drawing the copper wire in the works, taken around 1890. Useful on bad days in the office for reminding me of what my poor ancestors had to put up with!

This industrial rural power house did keep my ancestors employed long enough for national records to begin, and so those records were there for me to find. Today the row of workers' cottages they lived in are sold as sought after country properties, within easy reach of Alton Towers. The front gardens are long and thin, and I could imagine every inch would have been dug for potatoes and beans. But they are on the edge of the windy North Staffs moors and it still takes at least five minutes by car to reach the village of Oakamoor itself. On my first visit, as I stood looking at them, my only thought was what hell it must have been being in childbirth in such a bleak place.

Over a two day visit, I found pages of Swinsons in the phone book, dozens of Swinson gravestones and met the local headmaster who said he had several Swinsons on his school roll. Walking down the high street I saw several men who resembled my father and brother. What brought home to me just how long the connection of the Swinsons was to this land, was when I discovered in the local library that just a few miles away existed the town of Swinscoe, which had been a successful farming settlement of around one thousand acres established around three thousand years ago.

In my house in Edinburgh, I have a glass bowl full of Churnet Valley quartz stones. They are nothing special to look at, but for me they represent an important connection to the land where my forebears dreamed dreams, grew food and brought up their families.

This may seem absurd and fanciful, for I live three hundred

miles away, I have no close relatives in Staffordshire and had never heard of the Churnet Valley until recently. Yet this connection is real and in my blood. I feel earthed, in a way no amount of career or material success could achieve. Establishing this connection to the land has also radically changed how I view my allotment.

Now I value it far more, for it has turned out to be the powerful key to a new understanding of our island's history.

What does it matter that my small plot is rented, not owned outright? The feelings of ownership and possession for land were established in my ancestors' DNA for thousands of years, long before Norman land grabs, enclosures and the invention of title deeds, council planning departments and mortgage-lending financial services.

The enclosures were a big issue in Staffordshire from the 15th century onwards. The area was a hot bed of revolt in the English civil war, with Protestant peasants fighting Catholic aristocrats, with such ferocity that following the Restoration, a Grand Committee met at Stafford to sort out the natives. Long before this, one of the most formidable land grabbers in this area of England was one Bess of Hardwick, Madam Enclosure herself. She was the Countess of Shrewsbury and the mother of the first Duke of Devonshire and her progeny intermarried across the British aristocracy. Living here in Scotland, it is interesting to see patterns repeated across the centuries, in that it was a Marquess of Stafford who bought up land in Scotland. His family was later ennobled with the title of the Duke of Sutherland, of Highland Clearances fame.

The legacy of land enclosures remains in both Staffordshire

and Sutherland to this day – both areas remain bleak, under-populated and poor. Check out the trade press in community development and you will often see jobs going in North Staffordshire and in the area of Highlands and Islands Enterprise, usually funded by the taxpayer.

Time marches on, spring comes, and with it youth, opportunity and new beginnings. In the spring of 1860, aged 14, my great-grandfather William Swinson walked out of Oakamoor and like so many others, headed into Manchester to work in the cotton mills. Family apocrypha says he had so much raw energy he could operate two looms at once.

Two years later, the American Civil War disrupted cotton supplies and brought famine to Northern England, which became known as the Lancashire Cotton Panic. The London middle classes busied themselves raising subscriptions for the Deserving Poor who said their prayers and did not drink. Thousands were still left to starve to death in the streets. William did not wait for charity, and over the course of three weeks he walked to London, staying in homes of trade unionists on the way. On arrival, he took a job in the Crosse and Blackwell canning factory in King's Cross.

Later he married, had a family and set up what became a successful second-hand furniture business in Clapham Junction near Lavender Hill, which continued well into the 20th century. His eldest son set up a chandlery business in the City. Eventually the partnership of Meldrum and Swinson of Camomile Street EC2, became millionaire owners of the Essex Shipping Line Limited in the 1920s. William's younger son became a lithographic printer and, heading north of the river to St Albans, married a gardener's daughter, who never had a book out of her hand – my grandmother, Lila Mary Fisher.

Like millions of others, these were ordinary people getting on with their lives, but they still played their part, however small, in the economic history of these islands. Attention must be paid, goes the line in Arthur Miller's play *Death of a Salesman*. And it needs to be, by all of us. For if it is not, then we do not count and nor does our history, nor do the risks and sacrifices of our ancestors. Others are left in control, free to reinvent the past to their material advantage.

Look at your own family tree. When did the break come from the land? I always feel this question particularly strongly when I meet people with Scottish surnames and Lancashire accents. I always want to ask, where did your family come from before the Industrial Revolution? How would they have celebrated the coming of spring? What would they have planted? What would you feel if you could travel there and plant your two feet on that land?

Such thoughts may seem fairly irrelevant as we rush around. Most of us are urban animals and would loathe an agrarian life, however much we enjoy gardening, writing large cheques at Dobbies and watching old repeats of *The Good Life*. The reality of living 'off' the land, most of us feel, is best left to misguided souls on reality TV. Yet if we accept that we are what we grow, then we must celebrate the fact that deep, deep down inside, lies our ancestors' experience – comprising of not just what they grew, but where. In spring, when nature waits for us to start work, it is worth digging for that connection.

MARCH

Lights, Music, Fertiliser!

Curtain up in eight weeks. Hard to believe it, for right now my allotment is a frozen quagmire after months of wind, rain and frost. But even so, I am hard at work plotting and planning my next hit production – Allotment Year II. It is hard to imagine last year's profusion as I squash and squelch though the mud. But now I have all the anticipation of an empty stage four, a horticultural dramatis personae just waiting to be cultivated.

Though if I'm honest, it is comforting to see that the folk who acclaimed shows of flowers and veg back in the summer, now must deal with allotments looking just as depressing as mine.

I chat with a young allotmenteer three plots along and admire her artichokes. I'm not sure how to cook them, but in return for some green slime I bought to waterproof the sheds, she gives me half a dozen.

During this winter I have found that I could not leave my allotment alone, although the cold and damp of the river has limited each visit to about an hour. Apart from the blue and yellow paint on the fences, sheds and cold frames, my surroundings have hardly been flushed with colour. But I am astonished to learn from the City Allotment Manager that my painting efforts have so impressed passers-by that numbers on our site waiting list have risen from 12 to 54.

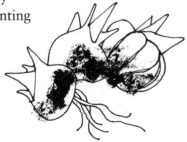

I spend cold Saturday mornings

painting inside the sheds while listening to Radio 4's 'Money Box' programme. It might seem like coals to Newcastle for a financial journalist to hear investment specialists pleading with the public to invest every spare penny in a pension fund, even though all our pensions are fast being reduced to anorexic slimness, plunging investor confidence and ridiculous management fees. How are all those shiny offices going to be kept full of shiny people drawing salaries, if suddenly the Great British Public decides there is more than one way to save for old age?

Perhaps one answer, besides proactive ethical investment of course, is to keep an allotment into your nineties, and be as self-sufficient as possible. In 1895, chocolate tycoon George Cadbury drew up the plans for Bournville Village for his workers, on calculations that an eighth of an acre with six fruit trees could keep a family of six all year. So why shouldn't a couple of pensioners manage perfectly well on 250 square feet?

As for the rest of us, whatever our circumstances, allotments provide a fun way to learn how to get by without spending money. Who needs to buy expensive plants when you can carry secateurs in your pocket and keep rooting powder under the kitchen sink?

Copying my more experienced neighbours, I now put out old manure tubs filled with nettles to catch the rainwater and make free fertiliser. I also gather seaweed along the beach when I visit friends – it's mineral rich and costs nothing. Also gratis, the council delivers leaves in white vans each Sunday afternoon, to lie and turn into mould. The driver assures me the leaves come from the city's cemeteries. Very organic.

But what to plant? The more catalogues I read, the more confused I get. I feel suddenly overcome with the same inadequacy I last experienced when I had my first baby. I read all those baby books only to feel I would never measure up as a new mother. So one day I binned the lot and from then on relied on good advice from experienced mothers. It worked for my kids, so perhaps my allotment could survive this approach?

I ring the people at the Organic Gardening Catalogue (www.organiccatalogue.com). They offer variety and reasonable prices, with none of the holier-than-thou moral high ground that many people in the organic business seem to think is a prerequisite. They suggest I should be propagating Brussels sprouts (Brilliant), early cabbage (Tundra) and even cauliflower (Mexico). They also tell me a great trick for peas: fill a piece of guttering with compost, plant peas along its length and keep indoors. When ready to prick out, make a furrow and slide the pea plants in.

Lights, music, guttering! As a weak spring sun warms the earth, I begin to feel my show really will go on.

Militant Gardeners Rise Up!

Saturday morning arrives cold, dreich and drizzly, so I head off to my local garden centre, where the staff know their horticulture, and deliver real added value, greeting me with suggestions for this column. After mooching about the seed potatoes – this year I have my eyes on Kepplestone Kidneys for an early main crop – I look around and realise just how much of this well-run garden centre is actually made up of expensive, pretend gardening items. Useless decorative watering cans, over-wrapped gift packs. I don't blame the owners, they have to make a buck in the Scottish climate, but the ersatz nature of the gardening business and the public's acceptance is depressing.

It's been getting worse for years with celebrity gardeners puffed up by TV and publishing spin-offs, but the way this has spilled into people's lives has gathered pace in recent years, to the point that gardening has somehow been reduced to spiritual junk food. How much mental space and peace of mind do we get from our bedecked, bepaved and bepotted gardens? Because if people are not out working to service the debt accrued in buying all the high-margin gizmos in the first place, they are slumped outside, burned out and knocking back the Chardonnay, looking at more bought things than nature. Whom does that suit?

Of course, nature has ways of lashing back. Not least in London, where paved gardens now cover three times the surface area of the capital's roads and are causing environmental damage as flooding becomes the norm. Water no longer soaks into the earth and into London's rivers, but rather runs straight into swiftly blocked drains.

Interestingly, there are early signs that human nature is on a backlash too. Wildlife has been in fast retreat but there is now blog talk of gardening guerrillas, fighting 'pave-overs' by throwing wildflower seeds over fences into the cracks between the slabs. Gardening makeover shows are being axed, and spin-off books remaindered. Even more interesting has been the public outcry – 98 per cent of correspondents to Radio 4's Gardeners' Question Time were against the BBC's rotten Chelsea Flower Show coverage in

2005, where egocentric presenters flirted to the camera, blocking the plants. This month council allotments lists will start to lengthen as people think about registering in time for the summer. For the priceless glory of an allotment is within its messy, *Cold Comfort Farm* joyous muckiness, which sets the spirit free, and can't be marked up and sold on.

Love Me, Love My Shed

'You do realise that most normal people would prefer to be in the South of France,' my husband commented.

It was a cold, very cold, March afternoon, and he and I were having lunch in my allotment shed, sheltering from the bitter cold wind and the snow, which now swirled around the plot. Inside, thanks to new roof felt, we were snug and warm with hot soup and cheese sandwiches. I considered his remark. Certainly normal people in my own corner of Scotland would be, if not in the South of France, at least out shopping or at home watching old movies or the racing from Wincanton. On the other hand, 'normal' is not a particularly useful term if, as I have long suspected, allotments are in fact a sort of *3rd Rock From the Sun* parallel universe.

And they're catching on. Allotment sheds have long been recognised as the last refuge of henpecked husbands; today they are increasingly popular among the hard-pressed female of the species. The reason, quite simply, is they are not normal at all, but magic. I had arrived that Saturday, ratty from the week's exertions, only to find myself fully restored when sitting on a stool in the shed. Does the magic have something to do with having one's very own shed? Do sheds tap into childhood memories of dens, treehouses, caves, hide-outs: secret places where we made plans, kept diaries and shared secrets, hiding from the grown-ups with our gang?

Now grown up myself, I have no way of hiding from any-one. Mobiles, text messages, e-mails, landlines and children pursue me into every corner of my day. So perhaps sheds turn back the clock to childhood.

I am not alone in feeling this. I have brought high-powered women friends down to the allotment to share a bottle of wine. Once they have stopped teasing me about my corkscrew hanging next to my dibber, my old past-it designer handbags being used as seed packet carriers, and

marvelling at the shed's general Second World War shabbiness, they relax and eventually confess to feel-ing a million dollars. Perhaps I ought to charge health farm prices?

Allotment sheds are a state of mind; their magic is unaccountable and therefore, as it cannot be counted, can bring infinite happiness. So, as I told my long-suffering spouse that snowy lunchtime, 'love me, love my shed'. Or, in the words of a Londoner walking past one day as I was painting the door, 'Blimey darlin', it's not a shed, it's a dacha!'

Let the Growing Begin

Whenever I invite people round for dinner, if I am lucky and well organised, there is always a brief moment before the doorbell rings, when I look around my home and actually appreciate it as a *mise-en-scène*. Just at that moment, it is as tidy and perfect as I can make it. Curtain up – any second now. Inevitably of course, the evening descends into a farce of dirty dishes and roaring laughter, but I always value the expectation. My allotment has now reached just such a moment. For weeks, I have been hoeing, composting, tidying, pruning and path clearing. All set dressing and stage management for show time, when planting starts in earnest and the hotter weather drives the weeds bananas. I am savouring the calm.

Perhaps it is only at these moments when we stop rushing around and take the trouble to observe our surroundings. The rest of the time, how often do we really give ourselves permission to use our eyes? I am now training myself to observe. On each visit to the allotment, I have come to realise how many tiny rites of passage I would otherwise miss: the extraordinary purply profusion of buds on the blackcurrant and redcurrant bushes, last year's daffodils making a sneaky comeback behind the trellis, or those secret red flashes of rhubarb stalks, too easily forgotten under their buckets. Look closely, and even compost bins are dramatic, in their own way. How quickly everything rots down, until thick, crumbly, black compost emerges from the bottom, which looks nothing like the fruit peel, old bread and last week's newspaper still lurking at the top.

I'm impatient for the season to start. For months now, during this long, cold winter, my allotmenteering has mostly been carried on indoors, at home. Pumpkins, courgette and broccoli have all been growing fast in heated seed propagators which occupy almost every windowsill. I have even indulged in a bit of one-upmanship and grown some Hensol Violets, a rare, new, perennial, purple poppy. But dinner parties? Forget it. Instead, I find myself shelling out rent to both my children, for propagator space on their bedroom windowsills. (Makes a nice ethical change from being charged usurious rates of interest for lending me their school dinner money!) As they have been brought up by a business journalist, I suppose I should not complain when they demonstrate such well-honed, commercial instincts. The little angels rightly point out that their windowsills are spacious, greenhouse hot, and face south. So I pay up. The show you see, must go on.

APRIL

A Chip Off the Old Block

Apart from a few wistful snatched moments between storms, my allotment and I have barely seen each other over the long winter months. What heartache. Yet strangely today as I reintroduce myself, tiptoeing round the plot, trying not to damage the soil structure post-frost, I feel almost shy. I remember a recent TV repeat of *Sex and the City*, where Carrie Bradshaw alias Sarah Jessica Parker, waxes lyrical about the sweet early courting stage when you have just started dating a new man, and, as you don't know anything about him, all is moon, June and Manhattan springtime. Oddly I recognise exactly how she feels. For with an allotment, every spring it's lu-rve. All the traumas last year over promiscuous couch grass hopping from bed to bed and those swine vegetables who treated you like dirt are but distant memories. This time around, anything is possible.

Obviously as with all new relationships, you vow not to make the same mistakes again. So this year to avoid any potential feelings of inadequacy, I am planting out one third of the plot with fruity bushes – blackcurrants – the Ben Alder and Ben Sarek varieties which give sweet firm fruit – and raspberries. Autumn Bliss is best for our climate, and don't need much support. The rest of the plot, which isn't already

colonised by the strawberries, rhubarb and my daughter's flower patch, is therefore up for grabs.

So I have decided to try exciting new varieties of a vegetable which everyone in the family eats. No, none of us are stick-thin like Carrie Bradshaw and we could never stick the Atkins diet either, so this has to be the Year of the Potato.

Some potato facts. We eat 6,380,000 tonnes a year according to the British Potato Council, but as with all relationships we have been in too long, potatoes are terribly taken for granted. Even though its very name is exotic. Derived from the native American Indian word 'batata', it was first cultivated by the Inca Indians in Peru over four thousand years ago. Grown ten thousand feet up in the Andes in poor soil, the Incas developed over two hundred varieties of a tuber which, living in the nightshade family (Solanaceae), has interesting relations – peppers, aubergine and tomatoes.

Potatoes are also nowadays written off as fattening – often by people knocking back fizzy drinks. Wise up! For there are two types of carbohydrates: simple carbohydrates found in refined sugar, sweets and most refined products which give a quick burst of energy quickly which then depletes just as quickly, and complex carbohydrates found in potatoes which releases energy slowly, keep the blood sugar level steadier, the body's best source of energy on a long term basis. Potatoes are also high in fibre, Vitamin B6, Vitamin C and Potassium.

And just to convince you further, may I mention these old remedies – treating spots on your face by washing your face daily with cool potato juice, or treating sunburn by applying raw grated potato. No, I haven't tried them either, but they do sound convincing. The joy of growing your own potatoes is getting away from the usual boring varieties on sale in the supermarket – your Desirees and your Maris Pipers. Yawn. One of the best catalogues around to feed your imagination is the Thompson & Morgan Potato Collection (www.thompson-morgan.com).

March is when early potatoes go in so this month I'm digging for victory with T&M's Second World War star variety Home Guard. Make a, ahem, trench, roughly 15cm deep and plant the potatoes roughly 40cm apart. They need to be earthed up about three times to encourage growth and stop small poisonous green patches developing. I forgot to do this in my first season and had too many green poisonous tatties to count.

Then later come the main crop varieties. This year I fancy that new tasty Irish spud, Rooster, currently the new love of top chefs across the UK (pale yellow dry floury flesh). But there is always the pull of the old varieties. I'm opting for Kerr's Pink, an heirloom potato, and staple of Burns Suppers everywhere. 'A man's a man for a' that', with its pink skin and tall robust foliage.

Then for the patriots among us, (alas, Thompson & Morgan have yet to get real about devolution) what about the Red, White and Blue Collection? Six tubers – two each of the three heirloom varieties: Highland Burgundy Red which gives you smashing burgundy red mash; Mr Little's Yetholm Gypsy, which has white flesh though the skins is literally dark red, white and blue in appearance; and finally, my daughter is in seventh heaven about this – Salad Blues. Billed as a possible Victorian Kitchen garden novelty, which produces spectacular blue flowers and blue flesh but best of all – for little girls of all ages everywhere – purple chips!

Horticultural Therapy

This morning I am, at last, getting one of my first real in-depth sessions on my allotment after months of rain, frost and ice. Finally! Sometimes I almost feel a phoney writing about my allotment when I can barely visit it over the long dark winter months, apart from brief encounters to drop off kitchen waste into the compost bins, or to tiptoe over the ground to avoid damaging the soil structure, to inspect how more delicate plants have fared in the Siberian winds.

Today however, spring flowers are in bloom, with my daffodils happily doing a Wordsworth in the wind. The river is high and the tide strong, and everywhere there is that indefinable smell of new life. I clear away growth from an old shrub and see green shoots. Garlic! I had forgotten it was there. How easy it is to forget the topography of my old friend.

How fantastic to be back in business. For months I have pored over seed catalogues, dreamed big visions and made battle plans. Yet four seasons on, I am no raw beginner. This year, I am choosing specific varieties for colour and flavour. For example, my French dwarf bean of choice this year is Hildora, which may sound like some Victorian governess in a novelette, but is in fact a classy specimen, sporting look-at-me yellow pods which I'll use in salads or cooked. As for lettuce, forget boring Little Gems, this year I am bringing out the old window panes for Amorinos. Under glass, these babies show off deep rich red leaves. Aesthetic and gastronomic knockouts, and importantly, resistant to mildew too.

Today, hoeing gives me time to think, and I am struck by just how much allotments have changed in status since I first received my key four springs ago. Back then, the council

waiting list was short, and allotments retained a laughably
ferret and flat cap image. How much ribbing I received
from people who at that time were busy taking out mega-
mortgages just to get a garden. But at £30 per annum,
frankly I am the one laughing all the way to the bank.
Perhaps allotments' re-rating is partly due to a profound,
almost subconscious re-examination of our links to the land,
possibly sparked by the growing national interest in organic
and 'green' living; or is it just that this stressed-out country
has finally discovered the joys of slacking, and cottoned on
to a rather good thing that has been lying undervalued
under its nose for far too long. Whatever the reason,
suddenly allotments are hot, hot, hot!

Allotments are even being taken seriously by our elected
representatives. One day I mentioned to a politician friend
that I wished we could beef up allotment legislation for
improved provision, protection and promotion. For on
both sides of the English/Scots border, the law has always
been conveniently woolly for the benefit of the landed
establishment, developers and councils. I thought he'd tell
me to lie down in a darkened room, but suddenly, whoosh!
Politicians' cross parties are now talking about an allotment
amendment for a new forthcoming planning bill. The first
Oral Question is being asked this week in the Scottish
Parliament. I might even sneak away from my word
processor to watch. Yet my worry is now, have allotments
suddenly gone posh? Alarm bells
recently rang when I received a
harrumphing letter from a man who
says that if allotments are so special, then we all ought to be paying
commercial rent on our land in the

city centre, or else means tested off it, with the land kept for
the poor. What a big hearted fellow he must be! Poppycock sir.
My view is that anyone without somewhere to grow fresh food
is poor indeed, whatever the size of their income.

Allotments of course now come under different names –
such as city farms or community gardens. And on these, there
is now a growing movement of something called Horticultural
Therapy. Now I have long realised that just hoeing for a few
minutes is guaranteed to take my shoulders down from my
ears, yet HT, as it is called in the trade, is big business. I
could take a course, or become a practitioner. And with GPs
now encouraging outdoor pursuits to beat mental illness and
depression, soon everyone will either be digging to be their
own therapists or else cultivating new careers to bring therapy
to someone else.

I am particularly taken by Thrive (www.thrive.org.uk),
a national charity which enables disadvantaged, disabled,
and older people to enjoy gardening. With 38 staff and over
one hundred volunteers, Thrive offers training, events and
courses, and runs four allotment style gardens, where small
miracles are allowed to develop. For example, for those with
literacy problems, gardening provides motivational reading
practice – such as reading seed packets – and concepts of
width and length are more easily understood when planting
out seedlings. Gardening for groups with special needs also
delivers social skills, and even roads into employment, while
stroke victims can recover movement by using specially
adapted tools, with boosted self-esteem as they see visible
progress as plants grow.

All in all, allotments are becoming really big stuff. Hence
why, you must excuse me, I am going to stop writing now
and crack on with my parsnips.

If You Can't Dig, Blog

What sort of person is an allotmenteer? Do we defy stereo-
types or do the nation's plots continue to be ruled by those
legendary flat cap-wearing grumpy old men? This has been
the latest hot topic on my online allotment blog.

I have always found the more experienced allotmenteers on
my site a huge source of advice and inspiration, flat caps or
not, and I tell my fellow bloggers as much. I add: they are
rarely grumpy unless foxes or vandals have done their worst,
in which case I, too, can grump for Scotland. What is
striking in the ensuing debate though is the age range of the
bloggers. There is the 13 year old workaholic who somehow
manages her plot while commuting over 14 miles to school,
plus assorted young mothers with children in tow,
traumatised after seeing *Jamie's School Dinners*. The debate
also reveals an interesting slant on fortysomethings'
relationships – some 'do it' with their partners, others to get
away from them.

For me, the joy of the UK 'lottie' community is, firstly, our
geographical spread, from Aberdeen to Torbay. Then there's
the range of our occupations, from a sound engineer in a
punk band to nurses, architects, scientists, joiners and, in
one case a barrister, who one night took his colleagues out
for an al fresco meal of oysters. 'The best part was when the
taxi drove us into the allotment; I think they thought a
contract had been put out on them.'

The hot topic this week is potatoes. The broad consensus
this year is: Charlottes for second earlies and Picassos for
the main crop, plus the less than tasty sounding Ratte.

Being allotmenteers, even online, there is naturally a healthy
one-upmanship. Newcomers naively ask whether they need

to leave potatoes to 'chit', or sprout, only to be informed
that they must leave all the shoots on if they want lots of
small potatoes, four shoots for medium potatoes and just
two shoots for big 'uns. Discussion ensues whether one
should chit in the sitting room, greenhouse or kitchen.
Or the bedroom if you are really passionate.

I am pleased to report that my own tatties are chitting nicely
on top of the dishwasher in my utility room, and any day
now I'll be back on my plot and back in business. And yes,
wearing my favourite flat cap too.

Battling Snobs of the Sod

One of the most comical phrases I encounter is, 'where
exactly is your allotment?' That delicious adverb 'exactly'
shows this is no honest query about geographical location,
but a wonderfully Hyacinth Bucket quest for social judgement. Yet as we know, allotments were created in panic by a
19th-century landed establishment who feared a French-style
revolution from the urban poor. Even in today's fierce market economy, we allotmenteers all pay the same rent to the
council, whatever our own or our plots' social indices.

This 'where exactly' question neatly illustrates the complete
futility of property one-upmanship. For our current overheated property market is based on a land bubble, predicated
on an artificially restricted supply of land. Yet we simply
don't see this bottom-line truth. Recently, a writer friend
told me an extraordinary story. One summer, while working
as a gillie, he frequently heard a term used by the county
land-owners, which, though he was Scots born and bred, he
did not know: The Frisp. Finally, in an unguarded moment,
his titled employer explained that this is actually an acronym:

Ridiculous Ignorant Scottish Peasants – replete with F word. 'So am I a FRISP?' my friend asked, astonished. 'Naturally, dear boy,' his lordship replied. The FRISPs it transpired, are people who slave away paying for ordinary family homes with gardens attached. No land you see, which can be carefully registered in offshore trusts and kept in the family.

Whatever the social milieu of our sites, we allotmenteers know our place. At least if we get our kids' names down early enough on the council lists – just as our leading landowners put their heirs down for Eton – we can guarantee them a plot. Sadly, however much our homes rise in value in the land bubble, there is no guarantee that the next generation will be able to buy homes of their own.

So we must learn to look at land in a new way, and consign silly 'where exactly' snobberies to history. For while middle class FRISPs are polishing social pecking orders, others are laughing all the way to the Cayman Islands. Recently, I bumped into my favourite university professor. A knowledgeable allotmenteer and highly decorated by the Italian government, he is revered by his Italian fellow plot-holders. We discussed the merits of waxy versus floury potatoes – currently I have both Epicure and Admiral varieties chitting away nicely. 'Antonia, the point about allotments,' he said, 'is not the size of your house or whether you are a professor or a dustman, but the condition of your spuds.' First class, commendatore. FRISPs of the world unite – for a man's a man for a' that!

In the Lap of the Gods

It is Saturday afternoon, the sun is beating down and after months of rain, my daughter Ella and I are on the allotment for some serious gardening. Birds, returning from the southern hemisphere, flaunt their arrival overhead, wheeling and squealing, while I am engaged in a so-called 'easy to do' idea, which I read in a magazine: Build Your Child Their Own Bean Tepee.

I should know better. As the black sheep of Val Singleton's sticky-back plastic generation, anything remotely crafty ends up in bits. Unsurprisingly, after half an hour, my creation resembled the Leaning Tower of Pisa more than anything respectably Native American. Still, I persevere. We're only talking bamboo and string – how difficult can it be?

Ella sits nearby, reading aloud to me the new children's version of *The Iliad*. When I was a child I loved those tales of meddling gods, hunky heroes and beautiful temptresses – but as an adult hearing them again, I realise how familiar all these characters are, how often they crop up in TV soaps and sagas. Hector's wife Andromache, who immediately hates Helen's guts when that rotter Paris brings her into Troy, is straight out of *Desperate Housewives*; Hera, Athene and Artemis, all froth with jealousy, and plots around that sulky, silly Achilles, are all naturals for *Footballers' Wives*. Black and white; crisis, catharsis. Just the stuff for good ratings.

Ella's book finishes with an airy observation that after all that sieging, nearly all the Greeks died on the way back. Perhaps that's just as well. After all that drama, Helen and Menelaus weren't exactly a *Wife Swap* success story.

Egoists and those with a natural predilection for exploiting others are not usually found on allotments, thank goodness. Such characters steer clear; there is nothing in it for them. For the triumphs and catharses on our plots are small and contained, our theatre of endeavour small, while our pleasure in the beauty around us is both practical and intensely personal. In a world of gesture politics, TV drama built on pointless rows and empty consumerism, the very shabbiness and mess of allotment sites are manifestos both of faith and intent.

Here, no politicians' promises of sunlit upland progress, nor vaulting hubris pierce our calm. What we notice as important are the cycles of seasons, nature's extraordinary renewing beauty and how very short the allotted time is which the gods give us to be with the people we love.

Time's winged chariot draws near. Slow down, please. How much longer will Ella want to stay, sitting by a leaning bamboo tepee reading me stories?

Silence Grows on You

Allow me to describe to you the sounds of an allotment. Whereas in other parts of our lives, sounds which we rarely listen to intently crowd in, on an allotment sounds are magnified and play a special part in the whole experience.

For example, on winter and early spring days there is the sound of traffic because the trees are still bare. Hardly pastoral, admittedly, yet this white noise reminds me that mine is an inner-city plot and summer is on its way. In spring one hears the sounds of fellow plot-holders sawing wood – the sound of nostalgia, instantly taking me back to childhood days when my father built me a tree house. Then there are the squeaks of wheelbarrows chugging to and from the leaf-mould bins.

There is bird song, too, as the mating season gets underway, though I notice that the crows who adopted the tree opposite my shed have yet to return. Now there is the banging of wooden stakes into the ground as plot-holders sort out fence boundaries and the swish of water into watering cans – water just switched on by the council in preparation for the growing season. Later in the year there will be the persistent buzzing of bees in the comfrey patch.

There are sounds you will not hear on an allotment. You don't get chatter. People, if they talk at all, will stick to conversations about what they are growing, sharing advice and tips. You will never get those chewy barbs of middle class one-upmanship which pass for conversation – about house prices or which school your kids go to. There is no place for egos on an allot-ment. Those sorts of people don't 'get' allotments, they'd rather joke about them. Indeed, plot-holders can work next to each other for years without finding out what each other does for a living.

You will also rarely see an iPod. Just the stress of choosing which of those thousands of tunes to play would eat into the pleasure of being on an allotment. I suspect iPods are for those wishing to tune out of life, whereas on an allotment you want to be at one with nature. If you hear a radio, it is almost always a match commentary, because plot-holders would rather be on their allotment listening to a match than yelling at the television or from the terraces.

Best of all, there is the sound of silence; not the Simon and Garfunkel download, but the real thing, into which real peace seeps.

A Hoe-down and a Ditty in the Open Air

D'ye ken McKinlay's secret still,
Where all good men may drink their fill,
And toast the lassies wi' a gill,
'Til their breeks start to leak in the morning!

Hoe, hoe, hoe! Singing ribald folk songs – and this I am informed, probably unreliably, is an 'auld Arran' drinking song – is one of the joys of allotment life. You can belt out those lyrics in the open air with no one to hear – hoeing in rhythm, if not in tune. Sung to the tune of 'Donald, Where's Your Troosers?' I can also thoroughly recommend this ditty for times off the plot when engaged in boring repetitive tasks. Washing the car on a Sunday, perhaps? (Should get the neighbours going.)

Hoeing is a big part of my life now the weeds are taking hold. This year I am determined not to be beaten. Little and often is my motto. That weekend binge – and I'm not referring to the McKinlay's illicit whisky stash here – is not an option. I am grateful to my plot neighbour, who, one day, seeing my amateurish efforts, showed me how to hoe properly. The trick is to work in patches, down and then up, going over where you've been. Then rake the soil over. Hoeing is satisfying, because you can cover quite a large area in just 20 minutes, if that is all you can spare. Changing from your office suit into gardening clothes for some early evening hoeing is also great for stress. Let's get a sense of perspective about tomorrow's presentation.

At a business enterprise workshop this week, I meet a fellow allotmenteer who runs a successful translation company. It is

early evening and we are in a fabulous venue opposite
Edinburgh Castle. Unexpected fierce sunlight is picking out
the battlements and the best efforts of the city council.
Wistfully, we look out of the window. He wants to be on his
plot, planting beans, while my high heels are killing me, and
what I wouldn't give to be off duty, protecting my luscious
red rhubarb from the slugs, which are marshalling earlier
than usual. Forgetting business for a moment, we mention
this shared passion to a member of our buzz group.
His expression – a subtle mixture of pity and, well, pity –
suddenly reminds me of that line in *Shall We Dance?* when
Richard Gere rushes into his law firm's reception area to
defend a colleague being ridiculed by the secretaries,
shouting, 'There's nothing wrong with ballroom dancing!'
Yeah, right.

All together now: repeat the verse above, con brio.

Men and the Art of Workplace Maintenance

My mobile phone rings while I am on the allotment.
Someone from a businesswomen's network wanting me to
give a light-hearted speech about how women can operate
effectively in the male-dominated workplace. What they
needed was lateral thinking. I had rather thought progress
had been made, though cases of discrimination in London's
Square Mile persist – something that should exercise the
minds of women investors. Still, I note down the date and
fee, thankful the efficient-sounding woman on the other line
cannot see that she is speaking to someone wearing grubby
gardening clothes.

Privately, I have long thought that management decision-
making and workplace mental health would be much

improved if staff spent 20 minutes a day on the office allotment as part of their contract of employment: plots could be
planted up on the roof or around the staff car park. Great
for stress-busting as well as team-building, as Mother
Nature is a great leveller. Sounds daft? Well, these days one
could imagine a cutting-edge management consultant with a
book to push, charging fortunes for such advice.

We hear a lot about our lousy work/life balance in the UK;
but the term always implies that the two areas of our lives
are separated by some Berlin Wall. Yet the interesting thing
about an allotment is that it is less a patch of ground than a
fluid, exciting, imaginative way of thinking, which unlocks
creativity, particularly when it comes to problem solving.

This morning I am planting a variety of squash seedlings.
Perhaps my favourite are Twongas, wonderfully exuberant
and pale blue. The very word sounds like a Caribbean cocktail
(the sort we would buy on holiday, girls, if we had equal pay).
Up they go, climbing that trellis as if heading for the board-
room. But for something bent and shaped like a question
mark, there are always trombolinos, best eaten while young.
While for eastern promise, nothing beats Turks Turban,
resembling rows of sleeping genies.

Squashes have great names. Try dropping Moschata
Muscade, Calabash or Marina di Choggia into conversation.
Might work in the workplace. If some guy is taking credit
for the results you have delivered, or is winding up your colleagues, or making stupid jokes, or does not appreciate your
business chutzpah, tell him to be afraid. Be very afraid. Has
he not heard of the Zapallito Family? Go girl, that corner
office has your name on it! You may or may not add that
these babies are acorn-shaped and dark green, with tender
yellow flesh...

Nostalgia Takes Root

Hurray! Bring out the steel band! My sweet potatoes have arrived. At present, the slips look a slightly straggly and will need potting up for three weeks. I can't wait. I have never actually been to the Caribbean but sweet potatoes instantly conjure up a very happy youth spent in London's Notting Hill. Remember the movie with Hugh Grant? Well, my little flat was about a minute's walk from where he spilt the orange juice over Julia Roberts. And yes, there was a travel bookshop at the end of the road. I even had my own key to a communal garden, where once a year the residents held a garden party complete with steel band.

I arrived there after the riots and before Ruby Wax and all the bankers moved in and it was all marvellous. With the Portobello market just yards away, I could live like a princess on four pence, with exotic fruit, vegetables and flowers piled high and sold by the bagful. The Barbadians who arrived in the area in the 1950s had brought their own marvellous cuisine, which mixing with the earlier established Irish and Spanish communities meant an exciting fusion experience of sweet potato conkie bread, tapas and Guinness. I would spend hours drinking cheap nerve-jangling Turkish coffee, watching this cosmopolitan world go by.

Today sweet potatoes are the staple of most TV cookery shows, but back then they seemed very exotic indeed. I learned to cook them the Barbadian way, parboiled and layered with onions in thin slices sprinkled with flour and black pepper and covered with loads of milk and grated cheese. Children should start on them young because along with the sweetness they are a rich source of vitamins A, C and B6, potassium, riboflavin and copper.

Two years ago I had some success growing the Beauregard variety but this year Thompson & Morgan have introduced a new strain with the not very exotic name of T65, which they promise is reliable, and heavy cropping. For our climate they suggest cultivation through black plastic or in large containers under glass. Sweet potatoes are actually not potatoes at all, but belong to the Convolvulus (bindweed) family. They can be trained up canes and the leaves and tips of young shoots can be cooked like spinach. Last time, I used a plastic polytunnel – which precious Monty Don would stand me in the corner for I'm sure. Back in my Notting Hill days he was known as the pushiest costume jeweller in London. He is now lording it round Herefordshire fighting polytunnels and I am growing sweet potatoes on my windy Scottish allotment. Portobello days are a world away.

A Lot of Learning

The best long term way to protect allotments from deep-pocketed property developers and supine councillors is to involve the younger generation early. So it has been great to see so many families with young children recently taking over new plots on my site.

My own daughter Ella has been allotmenteering for four years now, and has grown out of her own mini-plot to help with all the work. She still dashes off to play or steal into her shed to write stories, but she is a popular member of our allotment community.

However, seeing three year olds on the site the other day, started me thinking about how best to cater for them.

Older allotmenteers may hate the very idea, but with care
and preplanning, I do believe it is possible for everyone to
have a marvellous time, safely.

The first step is to give your child ownership of a piece of
ground. Let them mark it out, with painted bricks or shells.
Don't spend a fortune on special tools, just buy small
gardening gloves – available at most local DIY stores – and
give your kids an old tablespoon. Small children can be
kept absorbed for hours just digging holes. They also love
making slug traps out of yoghurt pots filled with Dad's beer.
The slugs die happy and what fun fishing out the dead
bodies can be. Let your kids get mucky.

Safety, of course, is paramount. So make sure everyone is up
to date with tetanus jabs, and watch out for sharp sticks and
barbed wire. Walk round your plot, as you would your own
home, looking for danger points. Nettles are great soaking
in buckets for free fertiliser, but make sure they are cleared
away before kids come onsite. Always keep cream on hand
for stings and cuts.

The trick is to keep children interested by letting them
do the activities they like. Ella has always loved hoeing,
whereas other children prefer digging. Given their own
plots, children can become quite territorial and take
enormous care, not just of the plants but of the aesthetics
too. One small child insists that all flowers in her bit of
ground must be blue and violet. Her mother wisely lets her
grow seedlings at home in a propagator, which she waters
after school. Ella loves trellis and climbing plants, so our
allotment has honeysuckle intertwined with brambles.
She also grows huge sunflowers which can be seen from the
gates when we arrive.

Children love secret places. Climbing beans are delicious eaten raw, but their foliage also provides wonderful privacy. Keep watercolours, paper and pens on the plot, and encourage your children to draw and paint what they see around them. Laminated into mats, these works of art make great family Christmas presents.

Another surefire winner is rhubarb. Children love tucking it up under buckets to force it on in spring, then uncovering it on each visit to check its progress. Once picked, making rhubarb crumble becomes another fun post-allotment activity. The only potential tantrum trap comes when you have to persuade them not to keep picking it after July, in order to keep the stock strong for next year. Get round this by investing in autumn-flowering rhubarb, which can be picked while the rest has 'gone to sleep'. Teaching Ella to make crumble brought home to me the underestimated connection between gardening and child nutrition. In the current debate about obesity and fatty school dinners, no one has mentioned the contribution school ground allotments could make. But follow the money: school lunch suppliers would not earn fat dividends for their shareholders doing that, and councils would promptly say they couldn't afford to employ gardening teachers. Far too much like hard work. Children can't vote, so are not worth it. Perhaps parents should start making a fuss?

The educational benefits are huge but arise informally. Time management and prioritising are obvious skills, given allotment trips with children usually have to be kept under an hour. But you can also teach maths too – get a ruler and let them work out the ten centimetre distance between seeds. Children also learn about seasons and learn to 'read' the weather. Then there is all the wildlife to observe at close quarters, from birds' nests, ladybirds and butterflies, to the arrival of wriggly red worms which tell you when the compost is ready to be spread.

Best of all, are allotment birthday parties. Ella's twelfth birthday party saw six small girls spending all afternoon playing with a wheelbarrow, and organising a barbecue of sausages and baked bananas with chocolate. 'Going Home' bags consisted of plant pots filled with bulbs they planted themselves, with freshly picked brambles. Afterwards, their parents told me that despite the absence of professional entertainers and disco music, their children all said it was the best party they had ever been to, and... when could they get an allotment? Pleeeeeeeease, Mum!

SUMMER

A CASE FOR OVERWHELMING ABUNDANCE. OR WHY YOU WON'T FIND BEIGE ON AN ALLOTMENT

THE REAL DEAL ON the summer allotment is both being and feeling overwhelmed. Or should that be perhaps: Over Whelmed. Not enough hours in the day. Too much to do, too little time. The sheer abundance of the produce which all needs picking and digging, washing and cooking. Help.

What a contrast to spring, and the pathetic wondering gratitude on noticing that a vine or a bush, which has looked half-dead for months, has somehow summoned the energy to sprout a shoot. Now in the summer, the allotment is a green tornado, sweeping every waking moment before it. I will not be overwhelmed this year, I decide with determination as I lie in bed in the early hours of the morning, picturing my plot in my mind's eye. I think of past articles I have written on time management. That old line: how do you eat an elephant? You don't, it's a protected species, dingbat, is the obvious answer. But in the expensive parallel universe of the management consultant, you eat an elephant with a knife and fork. Big problems need incremental, well planned, small solutions. So I lie there itemising tasks to be performed in small areas of the plot before falling into sleep.

Thankfully, dreams generally do not feature the most overwhelming element of allotments in summer: weeds. Gardens, if they appear at all in dreams, tend to feature Versailles levels of perfection, or Secret Garden profusion. In real life, of course, the weeds take over like unwanted aliens. The mares' tails, the couch grass and all those damn dandelions, which greet me mockingly with their yellow faces when I turn up after a few days' absence. Sucker! They can't all be used for tea, I can't keep them all. They have to go!

Why do weeds feed so effectively into the Protestant work

ethic? That guilt. The feeling in the pit of one's stomach in the face of any success as a gardener, that somehow we can never, ever do enough. Why me, I think as I hoe away, before giving in to the temptation of gazing over at my (retired) neighbour's weed-free paradise. Self-pity rules, just when I should be glorying in all this. How perverse.

I remind myself sternly that being overwhelmed by nature as opposed to being overwhelmed by thoughts of work and the office is just why I applied for a plot in the first place. As an ex-Anglican, I should surely know better than to be taken in by the Protestant work ethic. It is simply an ingrained cul-

tural response, designed to keep own-ers of assets rich and our ancestors in their place. The meek shall inherit the earth, rather than the oppressed inher-iting the land – a rather less convenient translation for the powers that be.

The 19th-century creed of 'Self Help' took off when Samuel Smiles wrote his bestseller business book, and built the industrial revolution. However, by the late 20th century it had also delivered the West's lousy work life balance. Smiles' origi-nal message, which linked hard work to an individual being supported by a strong community and extended family, has been progressively hollowed out by a secular global economy based on consumerism. I now decide to fight my unprofitable cultural conditioning by buying a couple of wine boxes and throwing a Weed Party, rather as my agrarian peasant ances-tors would have had fun with their neighbours getting in the hay. I feel better already.

Water is another overwhelming element of summer. Heavy dew in the early morning, and the greed for it as the hosepipe satisfyingly squishes over-parched and groaning bushes. We're lucky here in Scotland, no drought orders or stand pipes for us, but then we must have some reward for cold winds and endless winters. Insects are also in overwhelming abundance – an ever rolling Technicolor movie of baddies and goodies. Top baddie for arousing sheer naked hatred is the slugs. Surely the most vengeful Sicilian Mafioso could not revel in the sight of death more than I, in the contemplation of beer traps, full of bodies. Fantastico! I confess I find snails morally more difficult, because of their beauty. Who cannot be touched by that curiosity in the stretched necks and arched antennae of young snails on an evening out? Yet I cannot let them live if they go near my crops. Sorry, but this is war and I take no prisoners. The good guys are the bees and butterflies, and for them I keep a small mountain of comfrey near the compost bin. And worms. Bless them. They really do have the right work ethic.

Thank goodness the summer allotment *is* overwhelming. The trick is to recognise that precise moment of high summer, when you are so overwhelmed, when life is exciting and when the allotment needs your sweat and hard work as never before. Why is it that we are so often busy worrying or competing that this small truth slips us by? Why are we so stupid to allow it? The seasons slip, often long gone before we wake up and realise that, at *that* moment, we were at our zenith, at that moment we were at our most influential, loved, honoured, feted and celebrated. Why did we not enjoy the moment more? Why did we allow ourselves to be so overwhelmed?

As we grow older, so much of our life is spent on autopilot. Little surprises us, and we prefer not to be tested, too far or too much. We may become inured to disappointment, and to disappointing others, to knives in both the back and the front. We learn to avoid what we dislike, what we're not good at, what makes us feel inadequate. And imperceptibly we slip into a muted, unchallenging life of beige.

This is why allotments can be so useful. They become our primary colours, unlikely saviours which make us get our hands dirty. If we are lucky we can stay on and the summer will swing back again, we'll get another season. Perhaps there is something about the interplay of private space held in community with others, which makes allotments, as opposed to gardens, reconnect us so strongly to joy, despair, hope, possessiveness, hate, friendship, fury, fierce pride. And love. Not least for ourselves. That's why allotmenteers are perhaps the richest of all gardeners, because we are not alone, we are what we grow, together. How lucky too, to be reminded every day, that in spite of everything the years have thrown at us, we are still alive and have another chance.

Nursery Plants

June. One of the best months in the allotment year, with everything coming out, up or into flower. Talk of summer holidays concerns me. The idea of leaving my allotment behind for two whole weeks, just as it hits peak form, is anathema. Instead, I talk enthusiastically of budget breaks during the October half term when I know that I'll have only potatoes and pumpkins to leave behind. For at this time of year, I am mistress of my own urban paradise, a sea of green, edged by poplars, which lies between the town cemetery, the town river... and the town prison. What more could anyone want!

Year Two of running an allotment means no start-up costs and so I have been able to treat myself to an extraordinary collapsible fabric wheelbarrow. Known as The Wheel Easy, it has been designed by fellow gardener Jim Allsop (www.allsop.com) for easy lifting. Out went that cumbersome metal giant which took up half my shed, this new baby folds up flat and hangs on a hook. I have also almost recouped the cost in physiotherapy bills, because I no longer have to cart the weight of the barrow as well as the contents. Brilliant. Though one selling point which the manufacturers seem to have missed, is that it keeps children amused for hours – carting dolls about, capturing the local snail population or filling it with weeds at 50p a barrowful. And that's another great gardening tool: bribery.

Contrary to myth, children are welcome on allotments. In fact, my own plot would not be the same without them. Rory, my cool teenage son, though not an avid gardener admittedly, spends hours sitting in a deckchair reading novels aloud to me as I dig. He has eclectic prose tastes. Last year it was Iris Murdoch – I suspect luscious Kate Winslet's portrayal was a contributory factor – while this year's favourites are *Mrs Dalloway* and *The Hours*. Thank you, Nicole. What luxury being read to in the fresh air! This year, my daughter Ella is also the proud mistress of one of the two sheds. Now freshly painted inside and out, it is equipped with a table, chair, pictures and curtains.

Children and allotments. I can imagine the horror of purist allotmenteers who think children should not be seen or heard. But one big change which took place in the Great Plot Handover in March on my allotment has been the arrival of several young families. Toddlers and allotments do go together with a bit of preparation, and the advantages for family life are far greater than just fresh veg. So if you are thinking of signing up your family, here are a few tips from fellow parent allotmenteers:

- Give each child their own plot and leave them to it as much as possible. Radishes, mustard and cress are good standbys, and also sunflowers. The cheap trays of instant petunias and pansies make a great afternoon's entertainment.

- Note that children adopt different habits on allotments; for example, Ella would not be seen dead eating fresh vegetables at home – her mother could win *Mastermind* in food disguise – but now our nice neighbours have given her the run of their curly kale patch, she eats this raw in handfuls.

- Buy your kids their own gardening gloves. Some parents go in for individual tools, though as almost all children want to use yours on principle, this is a waste of money.

- Be boring. Keep tetanus jabs up to date, keep antihistamine cream for insect bites, plasters and other first aid essentials. Clear the site of barbed wire, glass etc. Even if your children are no longer toddlers, look at your plot as if they are – children on allotments regress!

- Check out the web for good ideas. For example, www.parentsplace.com/family and www.kidsgardening.com.

Digging Cyberspace

Nine years ago I left London to live by the seaside to enjoy my two small children and to write a novel, *The Cousins' Tale*, commissioned by Hodder & Stoughton. It was a sort of fairytale interlude, for at the time of day when I would once have been strap hanging on the District Line, I would wander along the beach picking up shells and inventing characters. One of my favourites was Lottie: a curvaceous blonde who first entered my story holed up from the tabloid press having seduced the handsome and semi-married Member for Bigneth and Mossop. I loved Lottie. She was sassy and smart, with great timing. Call me a buttoned-down Brit but I have never been able to write the sexy bits of my novels with a straight face, and sure enough Lottie gave great comedy. Every time I typed her name on my word processor I was giggling. She was just so naughty! The playwright Luigi Pirandello once said that his characters were 'less real but more alive', and Lottie certainly had more life force than almost anyone I'd ever met.

Now a lifetime away, living in a busy city with an 11 year old almost taller than me, when I type the word 'Lottie' on

my word processor I am actually referring to my allotment.
In the increasingly popular world of online allotmentspeak,
a lottie is your patch, the fountain of all fun and excitement,
where baddies are not imaginary designer-dressed Hugh
Grant cads, but flesh and blood yobs who trample over your
crops and break into your shed. A lottie is part of a very
special cyber universe, where one finds friends, lots of them,
ready to swap tall tales of passion, triumph and heartbreak.
Trust me, in no time at all, you are hooked (to the point you
might even put off going out to the real thing!).

So recently, one Sunday evening, having returned from
inspecting my nicely burgeoning brassicas, thinning out
my onions and hoeing round the blackcurrant bushes,
I came home and went online to visit my favourite site
(www.allotments4all.co.uk). Soon I was deep into Lottie
land, into an ever thickening plot about bark chippings.

Creative writing workshops always stress the importance of
a snappy title, and sure enough tonight's was a winner.
'Skanking from the Council!' For in this tale of economic
derring do, my cast of characters, apparently from sunny
North Tyneside, swapped stories about how they had
obtained free bark chipping from the council, only for another
character to complain that his daft council had dumped so
much of the stuff on the lotties that no one can park in the
car park. And by the way, his 'No Tipping' sign was now
standing proudly in a sea of chippings. Someone else
commiserated and offered a van to transport aforesaid
chippings, and so off we went again into more lottie chat.
Soon it appeared that no council would remain unskanked.
A very satisfactory conclusion for me personally, as my council
tax bill for a massive £1,803 had arrived in the previous
day's post.

Then up popped CD Scarecrows. No, not the name of the coolest new boy band, but these arrivistes are certainly making the traditionalist Lottie-land old guard froth. For CD Scarecrows draped across fruit bushes, apparently whirr away, catching the sun and doing the business. According to 'Teresa' who writes in, just hang them from bamboos stuck in the ground at angles and they swing and catch the light. '...adorn your trees with them (great home made Chrissy decs on my lottie!)'. And you thought all those thirty million copies of Elton John's 'Candle in the Wind' sold for Diana's Memorial Fund would end up in landfill? Oh, ye of little faith!

'Richard' replies with a new twist. 'CDs threaded through video tape work even better. Tied to canes up and down rows, the tape twists every so often and as the wind catches it, the tape hums and birds don't like it. New tape is better but old tape snaps at times,' but as he sagaciously observes, 'recycling is fun!' Then 'Emma Jane' writes in breathless prose that drilling holes in the rim makes CDs spin even faster, 'scaring the nasty birds *even* more!' And on cue – for as every novelist knows, too much consensus gets boring – 'Legless' crashes this oh-so-cosy chat room. 'I am now banning CDs from being used on my plot!' he fumes. 'The darn magpies are a pain! They dive from the sky chasing the spinning CDs and then sit in my apple trees pecking at them. They were meant to scare the birds away from my soon to be developing fruit, and all they seem to do is encourage them....' The hussies!

The point is, you don't even need to have your own allotment to enjoy cyber lottie land. Just as a good novel can transport you to Botswana or Hogwarts or 19th-century London, such is the vitality of the writing of these happy lottie holders, you really do imagine yourself visiting lotties everywhere from Worcester to Cumbernauld. Find yourself absorbed in the battle of the Easter Egg Hunts, or in the joy of baking that first crumble with lottie gooseberries. Share in the fun of learning how to make comfrey tea to break down compost, weep as vandals overrun a lottie heroine's patch for the third time in a month, only to end up admiring her subtle, effective, though probably illegal, plot for revenge. And then there is that tear jerking moment, when after years of apparently zero growth, a young lottie holder rushes home with his first spears of asparagus to eat fresh with butter.

 As one website motto reads, Life is a Lottie. Some days as I kneel on my pad, thinning out the mange tout, with the hum of bees in my ears, I am almost tempted to start plotting a sequel, invading my own original Lottie's smart and pristine Mayfair world – just to let her know how much she's missing.

Theory that's 'good enough' for my Sanity

Hot news on the plot this week is that the council allotment manager has just visited to judge the Best-Kept Allotment competition. Instantly, feelings of guilt, inadequacy, being cross with myself – yes, all the usual cocktail of female emotions – rise unbidden. If only I'd known. If only I had hoed more, made the place neater, planted more stuff. What must he have thought?

I have long considered that this automatic knee-jerk reaction, this unrealistic search for perfection, is woman's worst enemy. Why do we do it? Even after decades of earning money and running our own lives, why is achieving perfection still so central to our female identity?

What victims this makes us, how easily we're manipulated by commercial vested interests. Perhaps it has much to do with hard-wiring laid down in childhood, particularly if we were influenced by female relatives who were housewives in the 1950s, when wartime freedoms were withdrawn and advertising took hold of a deferential population, by then desperate for a better life, yet programmed to accept government propaganda. Domestic perfection through consumerism became the key to happiness, a false god that harried too many desperate housewives into being hooked on antidepressants, those 'mother's little helpers'. I can reason with all this. So why do I give a toss what the allotment manager thought?

Thankfully, a newer, stronger conditioning kicks in, one acquired in maternity hospital when having my first baby. In those days first-timers stayed in for a week, learning from more experienced mothers. My guardian angel turned out to be a weary lady on her fourth son. Firmly, she told me I never had to be the perfect mother, just good enough. Nothing more. The 'good enough' principle also applied to the cleanliness of my house and the whiteness of my son's Babygros. That way I could enjoy my baby and not give a monkey's what anyone else thought. Her other tip was to never buy baby books as they only leave you feeling inadequate – just observe children you liked the look of, and copy what their mothers do.

I have since applied this fantastic advice to every area of my life, including my allotment. So every season I note plots I like the look of and ask their owners for their advice. I learn fast, and own just one gardening book.

So now you know. The truth: my allotment is not perfect; nor are my children, my house, my ironing, my cooking, my flower arranging, my figure, my wardrobe and, if I'm honest, my working life. Just good enough. And that's OK by me.

A Man's a Man for A' That

What do you think about at the allotment? When I am asked this, I rarely know how to answer. Some days I work on problems, hoeing aggressively to get feelings (and people!) out of my system. Better out than in, as my granny would say! Other times thoughts drift, a luxury in a stressful world. Sometimes, I concentrate with an artist's eye on the saddle of a worm or a leaf, or even feel the urge to pray, allotments being very spiritual places.

One interesting development this year is that for the first time, my husband is getting involved. Ever since we met as students at Edinburgh University, he has never, ever once expressed interest in gardening of any description. Friends advise me to break out the Bolinger. But I find it slightly unnerving. Is this a mid-life crisis? Or a take-over? As a true Ayrshireman, in the past his activities have been limited to tattie howking, but now apparently a desire for exercise and mental space has made him pick up a hoe for the first time in his life. What a man, I tell him. Half an hour and a wash-board stomach is a dead cert.

So I now have more time for planting. The big excitement this year has been Thompson & Morgan's coloured cauli-flower collection: Orange Experimental, Emeraude (green), Aviso (white), Graffiti (purple) and Gitano (Romanesco). Cauliflowers are a bit picky about their soil and prone to pests, but with my man sorting out the weeds, why should I worry?

I arrive home from work one sunny Friday evening to find he has been at the allotment all afternoon – without me! Both children are draped artistically over the sofa watching *Hollyoaks* and waiting for their parents to provide the usual Friday night curry.

'So how did you get on?' I asked. ('How much did you do?' would have sounded a tad grasping after all.)

'I wrote you a poem,' he replied. *A poem!* That man never ceases to surprise me, hence why I suspect we are still married. And here it is:

Love at First Sight

Edinburgh's the brawest toon
It's where I met yir mither
I met her in a stairwell
How her presence made me shivver
Her long red hair cascaded doon
Like Rita Hayworth in first bloom
Her big blue eyes held out such promise
I knew the bells would ring out for us.

Talk about hoeing your way to a girl's heart. Who would have thought the spirit of Burns lives on in the 21st-century Ayrshire male! We ignore the sounds of faux vomiting coming from the other side of the room.

How to Know Your Onions, and Other Vegetables

I do believe there is a new mood abroad, a zeitgeist or spirit of the times. As the nation finally maxes out on junk food and credit card consumption, one can detect a new desire

for life to be real, to count for more than just objects for us
to buy. I'm calling it the New Authenticity. So the Turner
Prize nominates a painter, and allotment-style gardening
arrived at the Chelsea Flower Show. This New Authenticity
was also on display at the recent Gardening Scotland Show.
But here, going one better, were not just a few rows of veggie desirables, but an entire gold medal-winning allotment,
courtesy of Edinburgh City Council's Parks Department.
Bless them, they had reproduced rows of CDs hanging over
the peas and plastic bottle tops stuck over bamboo canes,
even a shed. It was perhaps a bit neat, but its design stood
out among the formal displays for a very different aesthetic,
powerfully challenging the pastoral and aspirational.

Among the show gardens another allotment, a Community
Garden, was being constructed in real time, to show the
public how to do it. Here the emphasis was on good mental
and physical health, and everything used had been recycled.
I particularly liked the way old tyres were used to keep
herbs in check.

Normally one expects pride of place in the Floral Hall to go
to the fanciest bonsais or the rarest orchids, but this year the
best-positioned stand had been given to the National
Vegetable Society, one of those invaluable, hidden gems
of civic life, which frankly anyone who wants to grow
vegetables well should join. Here, with their gold medal
certificate proudly displayed, was an astonishing array of
vegetables grown by amateur gardeners. Gringo carrots,
bottle-green Faulds parsley, and pale aristocratic Winston
potatoes, which apparently always impress judges, but make
lousy chips. With four thousand members across the UK,
around four hundred in Scotland, the Society is run by
gardeners for gardeners. The annual £11 subscription buys

access to a vast bank of shared knowledge, and rare varieties of vegetables never seen in garden centres. We are constantly told we live in a 'knowledge society', yet our masters tend to choose what is valuable and worth paying for, from a very narrow commercial menu. So in the spirit of New Authenticity, what price for the knowledge and passion of one Scottish member, who attended the Malvern Show last year with 630 varieties of potato?

Let's Have a Shed Summit

On 2 July 2005, thousands gathered in Edinburgh to march
and Make Poverty History, a remarkable event making
extraordinary global connections and political waves.
Yet what a chance the Make Poverty History alliance has
missed. For while concentrating on symptoms of global
injustice – unfair trade, aid and debt relief – they have let
the G8 leaders off the hook by ignoring the biggest cause of
global social injustice of all: land. Historically, it was the
invention of the limited liability company which provided
the mechanism for businesses to grow out of the corner shop
to global proportions, but it was the establishment of land
title in the West that, settling over time like good compost,
led to the creation of capital and to the genesis of the
market economy, the unchecked extremes of which we are
forcing political leaders to confront today.

Social injustice always starts with land: who grabs it, who's
kicked off it and who keeps it. In Scotland lack of security
of tenure caused terminal emigration, strangled enterprise
and the situation today where 350 people own over 50 per
cent of the land and 80 per cent of Scots are squashed on to
three per cent.

Let's look at Scotland's new partner in the developing world,
Malawi. According to UN figures, 85 per cent of unforested
land has 'customary' tenure vested in the president.
So people enjoy neither private property rights, nor security
of tenure. Eighty per cent of Malawi's population lives on
just 15 per cent of this land, in tiny plots, with the rest of
it doubtless divvied up among the elite. Yet if there were
international pressure for land reform, families could either

own land outright and borrow money against it to invest in their own business, or enjoy security of tenure so they could plan long-term.

Land justice must surely be the next campaign for the Make Poverty History alliance. And this time let's invite business to the party. Because surely the developing world itself needs to make poverty history – by minding its own business and making money. For this it needs security of tenure, the establishment of legal title to land and the development of responsible banking legislation to stop arbitrary repossession.

Perhaps Gordon Brown could rediscover his Christian socialist faith in co-operative economics? Perhaps Messrs Geldof and Bono could start emoting over land instead? Perhaps the First Minister could take some canny Edinburgh property lawyers along on his next trip to Malawi?

How about a summit in my shed to discuss this, gentlemen?

High Time to Celebrate

Most people have a summer 'Season', a series of fixed points throughout the summer which punctuate the precious short months when you don't feel foolish wearing shorts and walking around with a glass of pink fizz.

Years ago in London, when writing for a certain national tabloid, it was round about this time of year I would shamelessly rediscover my fascination for the corporate hospitality industry and would proceed to 'do' the Season: Ascot, Henley, Cowes… No bit of *Tatler* life was safe, for I had the frock, the hat and the press pass to match. When I moved back to Scotland, I carried on for a while in this vein. In fact, one year I actually found myself in the social pages of

Tatler, as a guest at a reception at Sotheby's sale of Scottish paintings at Hopetoun House. I was snapped wearing a sassy green dress and a big smile, having just bought a Robert Noble. Memorably, the following week, a London magazine editor rang, her first words being, 'Darling, we thought you were dead!'

Nowadays the joys of the summer season hold a happy allure which would make my younger self blanche. My season starts with the fantastic Gardening Scotland show held each June in Ingliston. The mini gardens are a real must to visit and the plant stalls in the Floral Hall very hard to resist. This year I came away with five different sorts of basil – including the purple Dark Opal Basil which gives salad and stews a marvellous spicy bite.

Then come serial BBQS, right through July, picking produce as we cook, followed by August with the annual Flower Show in Ayr's splendid Rozelle Park (www.ayrflowershow.org) and the Edinburgh Festivals, which if you are not careful, are prone to take one's eye off the ball when it comes to that all important end of summer event – the Allotment Show!

One key summer highlight of course is my birthday – as a Gemini my husband says he gets two women for the cost of one! This naturally involves judicious amounts of pink fizz down at the allotment with a gang of kindred spirits, for summer in Scotland must be the season for repairing the friendships we neglect when hunkering down in winter. This year, to add a bit of tone to proceedings I wore a flaming pink Philip Treacy hat along with my T-shirt and shorts. I had bought it for my brother's wedding, only to find that the lovely girl he was marrying had chosen a Quaker ceremony and hats could not be worn. But heh, if you've got it flaunt it. That's the great thing about an allotment Season, nothing is ever wasted.

Gardener, Heal Thyself

As someone who has spent the last four seasons energetically hoeing mares' tails out of their plot, it comes as a shock to learn that I am wasting one of nature's best beauty treatments for skin, hair and nails. This wayward plant is bursting with silicon, so snip a piece into boiling water, and make the infusion into tea.

This is just one of the fascinating pieces of information I learned at the one-day Herbalism for Women's Health course at the Four Winds Inspiration Centre (www.four-winds.fsbusiness.co.uk) in Edinburgh's Inverleith Park, a gem of a place for anyone with a practical interest in nature. Our professional herbalist instructor walks us round the garden as we frantically scribble notes. What an eye-opener.

I soon realise that my allotment is a fantastic free medicine chest. Take comfrey: it is an anti-inflammatory which repairs cell damage. Put the blue flowers in the bath, or drink the leaves as a tea. Raspberry leaves are great for congestion, while those nettles towering over my compost bin are the best blood tonic money can't buy. The roots, crushed in a tincture, are great for the prostate. And weeds are not weeds at all. Dandelion leaves are rich in potassium and can lower high blood pressure, while dock leaves shredded sparingly in salad help cure constipation.

As for sticky willow, get out the gin and make a tincture. Its proper name is Cleavers and it cannot be bettered for cleaning out the lymphatic system. Culinary herbs are also free medicine. Rosemary really is for remembrance; drunk as a tea it improves concentration and can also help with extreme grief. Lemon verbena lifts low spirits, sage tea cools hot flushes, and oregano tea works for PMT. I suddenly see another world growing all around me that I have been missing – or perhaps have been programmed to miss.

The medieval witchcraft trials across Europe cost the lives of several million women. This was primarily a male backlash against growing female economic independence based on administering herbal medicine, which challenged religious and commercial economic interests. Now I learn that what was also lost in the flames was huge knowledge, not least written knowledge, the loss of which has contributed to ingrained western cultural ignorance of the natural world. So while Indian and Chinese systems of herbal medicine flourished, European herbalism, which was based on the humours – the choleric, phlegmatic, melancholic and sanguine – was almost wiped out. Whom did that suit? Follow the money.

You Can Beat a Bit of Bully

The sun is beating down on my allotment. In front of me rows of sweetcorn are waving in the wind. Lettuce, celery and broccoli are equally abundant. Even my kiwi has eight blossoms on it – confounding all those pessimists who said it would never last a winter. I'm feeling pretty good about my gardening abilities until I see a neighbour's plot. Everything is gorgeous and greener and twice the size of my own horticultural efforts. Luckily my neighbour is a born teacher and gives me a free gardening lesson in how to make your own comfrey fertiliser in a barrel. What you do, is cut down the comfrey (leaving a bit for the butterflies) shove it all into a barrel, cover and leave until the vegetation turns black, then cover it with water and leave to 'stew'. You then drain the resulting thick black liquid into a plastic container, and

add just one capful per gallon of water. No more than that
or else it burns the plants.

Such kindliness is all part of the joy of being in an allotment
community. It suddenly occurs to me what an oasis of nurture
allotments are, in a world where bullying is increasingly
admired, and in popular culture, even revered. A few years
ago, the put-downs and rants of people like Alan Sugar and
Gordon Ramsay would have seemed weird, even antisocial.
As a business journalist, I interviewed far more successful
entrepreneurs than Alan Sugar, who stressed how treating staff
well impacted on the bottom line. And though the catering
industry has always been riven with bullying, since when was
this classed as entertainment? And then there is the much more
subtle bullying of Trinny and Susannah which is, as one would
expect from the female of the species, so cruelly on target.

This cult for TV bullying is particularly strange, because we
live in a time of far greater openness about mental health,
and far more employer litigation. And in an age of self-help
and doing it for ourselves, how odd that we allow such
top-down attitudes to make prime time. These bullies
operate under the guise of helping people. But bullying is
still bullying, however big their contracts. The real tragedy
of the TV schedules is that in offices, schools and homes
across the land, inadequates take this as permission to make
other people's lives a misery. Society is then left to foot the
bill. So while the living is easy, switch off those TV bullies,
get outside and start chopping down that comfrey.

To Eat or Not to Eat

Miracles do happen! While I am living proof that allotments
can transform quality of life, family diet, recycling rates and
unlock a whole new set of friendships, I have not yet
trumpeted from the rooftops the real miracle. The fact that
after years of indifference, I have at last become a good
cook. No, not a great cook, I know my place. Not some
domestic goddess dripping with luscious buttery adjectives,
but just a good cook capable of making organic, tasty,
everyday food for my nearest and dearest. Which gets eaten!

So what has effected this transformation? I think it has
everything to do with the flavour of allotment-grown food.
How hard it is to feel excited by cooking, when everything
you buy in supermarkets tastes of nothing whatsoever.
Or you need a second mortgage to shop at the local deli.
Or the corner shops nearby make a point of seeing how far
past the sell-by date they can flog their stock, in a new form
of merchandising machismo. The cumulative effect has been
that over the years, apart from brief holiday respites on
mainland Europe, I have become less and less interested in

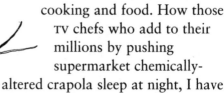

cooking and food. How those
TV chefs who add to their
millions by pushing
supermarket chemically-
altered crapola sleep at night, I have
no idea. As Joanna Blythman reveals in
her book *Shopped: The Shocking Power of Britain's
Supermarkets*, much high-margin processed supermarket food
is manufactured in the same factory, whatever the branding.
Meanwhile, we are reduced to buying an ever narrowing

and prescriptive range of fruit and veg, almost 50 per cent of which contains pesticide residues, chosen for storage rather than taste.

But with an allotment, once you get the hang of how to grow the fruit and veg, suddenly tastebuds start coming back to life. Take rice. Boring? Not if you add flavour and visual excitement with fresh marigold petals, sprinkled on instead of saffron. As for garlic, my own home produced variety has cloves the size of grapes and packs three times the va va voom of the shop bought tiddlers. Dug up whole they are the size of small grapefruits. Cauliflowers too, are perhaps traditionally more redolent of school dinners than the candlelit variety. But just try growing your own, and serving au gratin with hard boiled free range eggs and anchovies and watch as your vegetable-hating children ask for more. Or try them on spinach freshly cooked with butter, black pepper and lemon.

Fancy rhubarb crumble which actually tastes of rhubarb as opposed to plasticised goo? I kept my rhubarb covered by buckets for most of the winter and early spring, dividing the crowns. Conventional wisdom is that you should not pick too much from divided rhubarb but with allotment rhubarb, the more you pick the more it thrives. Hence my new culinary line of rhubarb and orange crumble with ginger. I recently fed this to the poshest people I know and saw them thank me with tears in their eyes as they asked for 'thirds'. For the fact is, tastes and smells carry our earliest memories, and for anyone over 30, tasting this food is like the eating of one's childhood, before the days of mass supermarkets.

Another spur to my cooking has been growing herbs, not just the usual parsley and rosemary, but more unusual herbs, many of which have an historic, even literary past, adding old flavour to modern dishes. Those wonderful blue flowers of the borage plants (*borage officinalis*) are a wonderful bee magnet. But did you know that the word comes from the Celtic *borrach*, meaning bravery. An infusion of borage was given to the Crusaders before they set off. In Shakespeare's time it was sprinkled on cider, while today it's a must for a jug of Pimm's. Then take basil (*ocimum basilicum*), for a bit of grisly drama. My own bushy plants wave happily in their sunny corner next to the compost bin. Yet what a role this humble annual played in 14th-century Italian writer Giovanni Boccacio's bawdy *Decameron*. How 'Corrie' scriptwriters today would love the storyline of the beautiful Lisabetta whose lover Lorenzo is murdered by her brothers. When Lisabetta learns from a dream that Lorenzo has been killed, she finds his body, and puts his head in a pot of basil. A novel way of keeping your man where you want him.

As for a more romantic perennial herb, how about sweet violet (*viola odorata*) which thrives in sun or partial shade and fertile moist soil. This is tasty sprinkled on salads, and I remember my grandmother crystallising her own violets for our birthday cakes as children. And what a sexy provenance. It was sweet violet which formed the basis of the magic love potion made for Queen Titania in *A Midsummer Night's Dream* which caused her to fall in love with the first creature she saw on waking up. You may remember this turned out to the 'rude mechanical' Bottom wearing a donkey's head. The recipe was revived by the Royal Chemistry Society on Valentine's Day 2002 to coincide the Royal Shakespeare Company's production. Like all the best stories, its efficacy is debatable, but should you see the man of your dreams across a crowded plot, it might be worth a try – before you further enchant him with your rhubarb crumble, that is.

In Pursuit of a Silver Cup

I wonder sometimes if my beloved husband 'gets' allotments. True, he once gallantly repaired my shed roof (to get out of doing tax returns). And occasionally he comes along to read the Sunday papers while I dig. But the gentle nuances of allotment life elude him.

Picture the scene: early weekday morning. I am getting ready for work, he is lying in bed contemplating a day off while looking at the post, quite the most important item being the catalogue for the forthcoming 53rd Annual Flower and Vegetable Show of our city's allotments.

Him: 'So how are you going to play it this year? The silver cups? A wee triumph. What's your strategy?'

Me: 'Er. Haven't got one. It's the taking part, isn't it?'

Him: 'No, no, no! You need a plan. Devise a strategy. You get a cup if you get loads of firsts and seconds. Look. You've got one month. Let's go through the categories, rate our chances and prepare!' (Note the 'our', gentle reader.)

'Potato Collection: Any Three Varieties'. No Problem. 'Salad Collection: Show on a Dressed Tray'. In the bag. 'Any Other Flowering Plant'. Mine for the taking. 'Class 86: Collection of Herbs in a Vase'. Points make prizes!

Mixed-race marriage discussion then ensues on how to pronounce 'vase', but the bottom line remains: I am married to an alpha male who hasn't recovered from last year's sorry truth that his wife came only second in the Rhubarb Class 103: Six Stalks. Nor the fact that she was thrilled.

Down the list 'we' go, from Vegetables into Flowers and Fruit and Floral Art. I am exhausted, convinced I won't have

time for a summer holiday. Daughter is summoned.
Children's Section. Class 100: Veggie Monster? Move on.
What about the adult sections? Boost the average. The family
honour's at stake.

'But she's only 12!'

'Class 126: Any Embroidered Item, looks promising. What
about that old tapestry on the wall. She could take it out of
its frame. Stick it on a cushion...'

'I can't do that, Dad. It's old. And anyway, I didn't do it!'

'Silver cup, yes or no? Class 99: Decorated Biscuit With A
Scottish Theme. I can think of one. Winning!'

That evening we go to the shops and he asks where the baking
section is. He is planning scones. For Class 105: Four Oven
Scones on a Plate. Never made them in his life.
Wouldn't know what's in them. No idea
how the oven works. Light and fluffy,
apparently. The texture just needs
practice...

Note: Come Show Day, we found ourselves on a trip to the Outer Hebrides, so
luckily – or not – there was no need to add silver polish to
the shopping list.

Plot on the Landscape

'Why don't you write about the allotments in *EastEnders*?',
I am often asked. Given its enduring popularity, the regular
scenes at the Bridge Street allotments must count as the best
advertisement for allotments in history. Yet I suppose I have
always found it hard to suspend my disbelief, because when

EastEnders first started back in the mid-1980s, an old friend of my stepfather, actress Anna Wing, was cast as Lou Beale, Arthur Fowler's mum-in-law. Anna herself had been brought up in the real East End and described it as harsh and hungry, not at all the chummy knees-up place of legend. And exciting though all the press hype and attention was, back then for the original actors, *EastEnders* was just another job with a tiring commute to Elstree, which may or may not last the year.

However, over the years I have noticed how well the Fowlers' allotment has thickened plots for the scriptwriters. You may remember when Martin tried to grow those dodgy plants, only for the Drug Squad to get wind of it, and when Jamie got the old graffitti can out and sprayed the sheds and Janine knocked back vodka. More recently, and it had to happen of course, sex finally arrived on the plot, courtesy of Mo and Bert. Say no more, squire! Next up – childbirth and a spot of sado masochism? Basically whenever the scriptwriters want to get the characters out of Albert Square, it's off to the allotment for a bit of 'how's yer farver?'

The big plus, however, is how much the show has boosted the popularity and profile of UK allotments. For example, Rowley Fields, Leicester's largest allotment club, reports in its online newsletter booming numbers, as young women apply to live the Fowler dream. I do wonder if they realise what they are letting themselves in for. Ongoing plotlines in allotment life may have definite element of comedy, bathos and drama, but alas, no minion from the Props and Set Design is going to help out with those weeds...

The *EastEnders* phenomenon has also spawned interest in academia. Online I discover a thesis outline from an American student with the catchy title 'Cockney Plots: Working Class Politics and Garden Allotments in London's

East End, 1890-1918'. Apparently East End allotments not only succeeded as a source of food during periods of sky high food prices, but also formed the seedbed for mass political activism. Gordon flamin' Bennet! Given our politicians are always bemoaning the loss of interest in politics among voters, maybe increasing allotment provision should be included in all party manifestos as we head towards 2007's Holyrood elections?

A Healthy Perception

An abundant jungle. This is how my allotment greets me after two weeks in bed with acute bronchitis. Raspberries, blackcurrants, early brambles and blueberries hang heavy on the branches. Ripe sweetcorn, now over five feet high, wave brown tassles in the wind, while potatoes, celery and French beans beg for attention. Weeds, huge ones, are everywhere. Thankfully, my box beds have kept a semblance of order and soon with some detemined hoeing, the jungle retreats. I pick fruit for the freezer, clear away the finished broccoli and start winter planting: tatsoi oriental leaves, giant winter spinach, leeks and a row or two of delicious Norli peas.

After a while, however, I start wheezing and have to stop hoeing. When a neighbour comes over to chat I sound like Fenella Fielding breathing helium. I am rarely ill, so it seems very odd to have been out of circulation this long. Just what a source of real wealth good health is! Yet how often do we take it for granted, forgetting to factor it in as an asset on the credit side of life, rather like unearned income on a forgotten account?

My neighbour agrees, and says that years ago allotments played a vital role in keeping poor families healthy at a time when many went hungry. He and his brothers drank cabbage water each day from the plot-grown cabbage and thanks to their plot, ate just as much fresh food as the rich families who had kitchen gardens.

One consequence of being ill in bed for days, is that I found myself watching far more TV news than usual. This daily diet of spiralling war, petrol prices, interest rates, bad debts, tsunamis, terrorist plots and airport mayhem made me think seriously about just how vulnerable families are becoming to new forms of poverty, however prosperous their standard of living. For success in the market economy apparently no longer guarantees personal safety, mobility, freedom from a credit crunch or the effects of global warming, let alone good health.

Is it now time to re-assess the long accepted norms of post-war prosperity? For as the West jitters and commodities soar, how will UK patterns of diet, leisure, housing, work and travel be affected long term? 'The Development of the Credit Economy in the West, 1946–2006'. I can already see this title for a future university course. It seems we are entering a new super cycle, so bottom line we must look after ourselves and each other, cultivating wealth in new ways. How extraordinary it would be if our remaining allotments, providing locally grown food and healthy recreation within close knit communities, should become the 21st-century lifestyle must-have for the lucky few?

AUTUMN

SEIZE THE DAY!

GARDENING PROGRAMMES AND gardening articles at this time of year always seem to start with the same phrase: 'Now is a good time…'. This is a really irritating, maiden auntish phrase which editors should ban. There is a chivvying, goading, world-weary, guilt-inducing tone about this line which we should all ignore on principle. Let me try this on for size. 'Now is a bad time to…, a fun time to…, an inconvenient time…' No I don't like those either, because they are just as prescriptive and hectoring. My time is my business and I'll decide what to do with it, and the adjectives to apply.

Bottom line, of course: autumn is all about time. It is THE season when time starts to race, almost as if we know instinctively in our marrow, from ancestral experience, that time is running out. Time for growing, harvesting or planting is running out, winding down. On the allotments we potter about planting parsley and autumn onions but with too much time to think perhaps, we can't help dwelling on the time. We lose track of it at the allotment but it's still there. What's the time? How much time do we have? How much time do we have left? Seasons of life. Take in the orange and yellow leaves on those trees before they blow away. Take in the purply blue of those Michaelmas daisies, the smell of the bonfire smoke, and the leaf mould before you leave. Take it all in. Gather in your harvest and enjoy every moment. Take in the red poppies on people's coats in late October, shorthand for lost time and wasted young life. Hurry, hurry, hurry before… Now is a good time…

When they think of the poet John Keats, most people think of 'Ode to Autumn', but for me his best lines are these:

When I have fears that I may cease to be / Before my pen has glean'd my teeming brain, Before high-piled books, in charactery, Hold like rich garners the full ripen'd grain;… –

*then on the shore / Of the wide world I stand alone, and think
/ Till love and fame to nothingness do sink.*

He died at 26. There was never enough time for Keats to
write the poems he wanted to get out on paper, to read all the
books he wanted to read. Note the harvest imagery. It must
have been an instinct.

Some people have this very strong instinct that they won't be
around long. One of my first jobs in journalism was writing a
column for the late lamented *Chat* magazine titled 'Where Are
They Now?'. This involved racing round the home counties with
a young photographer in his fabulous open-top sports car digging up former celebrities. I'm afraid our irreverent name for
the column was 'We Thought You Were Dead'. No one-hit-
wonder was safe. Remember Clodagh Rodgers, she of the micro
miniskirt? Or Julie Rogers of *The Wedding* fame? We tracked
them down. Peter, of Peter and Gordon, was discovered selling
mobile phones the size of bricks in a warehouse outside
Daventry. Then there was Frank Ifield, Ronnie Carroll, Mary
Peters, Twinkle. Terr-er-y! Time had gone on for them. Some
had built full and happy lives, others had never recovered the
loss of fame and suffered the poverty of celebrity: they were
still defined from one short season in their lives not just by
other people, but far more importantly by themselves. Did
they think they were dead? They must have or they would
never have touched our silly little column with a ten foot
barge pole.

I digress. As I say, some people have a sense that time is
precious and must be grabbed. And this applied to the photographer Edward Henty. I'll never forget him. He was a very
talented, attractive man from a rather distinguished family,
whose ancestor founded the first white settlement in Victoria,
Australia. What struck me even then back in the mid-1980s,
was that though Edward was only in his twenties he was

already married and a father and worrying about school fees. Children were not on my horizon; for me it seemed there was all the time in the world. 'Why are you rushing?' I asked him. What's the big hurry? If you have your children young, you have more time to play with them, he would say. A few years later in 1993, his name flashed onto the news. He had been blown up by the IRA in the Bishopsgate bomb which blew up the Baltic Exchange. He had gone into the area against police advice because that night he'd been doing an extra shift for the *News of the World*. To pay the school fees I bet. He was just 34. He must have had that instinct which measures out time and rushes on to complete, maybe he had needed the Henty name to carry on, beyond anything.

As a child, after my own father's death, my mother used to like me to sing 'September Song', that old Kurt Weill number made famous by Walter Huston. I always found it a really odd song, I couldn't understand why she liked it so much, it was so depressing. It seemed to carry such ersatz emotion which had nothing to do with me, but although I had a good strong singing voice, my own inner voice was a very fragile plant. That line about days dwindling down to a precious few. I could see the alliteration of the 'd' was effective but I never understood it, though I was too polite to say. As for the line about autumn weather turning the leaves to flame, I did not catch the nuance about that one last rush of desire. And I certainly didn't connect the song at all to my father's death from a heart attack in Spain. He was only 55. He should have lived much, much longer. It was absurd that the ambulance took hours to arrive. He was a writer with so much more to write. Now I wonder whether he had felt like Keats and had crammed in so many books and plays in the time available? In recent years, I have lost good friends to illness, two to suicide, and I have seen that life is messy and death even messier,

and at last now Time is working its magic on me. I am not
immortal. I have to plot and plan through life's seasons. When
autumn turns the leaves to flame, *carpe diem* I say. Seize the day.

*   *   *

I suppose it is a test of how much *carpe diem* we have achieved
in our own lives by how often we say to our children, I could
have become a painter/dancer/writer/singer if... The straight
answer to that is of course you didn't. We either had a go or we
did not. Life has a pretty unforgiving balance sheet.

I did have a go, though of course there is always a price to
be paid down the line, in the houses you didn't buy which
then zoomed up in value, and the money you didn't make.
Nevertheless, it was still a good go. For me, having a go meant
working 'in the business' with a real Equity card, on TV, and
radio, and in the theatre, learning to work an audience, not fall
over the furniture, timing a line. This early work experience
comes to my rescue every time I have to stand on a platform and
make a speech. I learned how to fall back on the audience's
goodwill and work it, like a child learning that the water will
beat them up when they swim.

Then came journalism, an absorbing career which lasted on
and off for two decades. After serving my time on *Chat* magazine
I finally arrived on Fleet Street writing for the nationals. I
wouldn't have missed my first days on those last days of Fleet
Street, for anything. I arrived in 1987 at a time when Margaret
Thatcher was Queen, Princess Diana was every hack's fairy god-
mother, and Eddie Shah was a provincial newspaper owner
few people had ever heard of. The Black Lubyanka, as the old
Express building was called, was a throbbing hive of Spanish
practices and newspaper history. We would rush around dusty
corridors, not bothering to look out grimy windows, still car-

rying the marks of wartime black-out tape, and talk in hushed tones about an exciting new machine called The Fax, which apparently lurked in splendour in the editor's office, though few had seen it. Bromides had nothing to do with what once was put in soldiers' tea, but were multiple carbon copies for the sub-editors and printers. The two bottle, two hour lunch was pretty much the norm, and by 4.55 if your copy was not on the subs' desk, the air, as one old Scots hack described it to me one day, turned blue with blasphemy!

I was very young and very cheap and soaked up knowledge like a sponge. Pretty soon, I was given my own column every Friday, a one page mosaic of titbits rejoicing in the name of Hot Properties. What's hot, what not! What's in, what's out! Oh yes, the *Express* was turning hip and trendy for a younger generation who wasn't buying it, while thoroughly perplexing good people like my Auntie Muriel who did. 'To Bonk' was the verb I had the honour of breaking officially to the *Express* readership as the new 'in' slang. As I tell my children, we were but a simple people.

Still, what a way to earn a living! My friends and I would stay in the pub drinking until ten o'clock came, when we would run down to the street at the side of the building, where lorries would be loaded with stacks of papers. Some of the bails were intended for the main stations and nearby hotels like the Savoy. I would grab a copy and take in the warmth of the paper, the black and inky smell of the newsprint and stand in the semi-darkness rippling through to see what had been done with my words written that day.

'It should be called the Daily Swinson,' one of the older subs once joked, so prolific was my contribution to the paper's word count. I had all that infinite creativity and raw energy you have in your twenties. How I wish I had valued it more, or could have kept some stored up for later.

This was the heyday 1980s when the Hooray Henrys in red braces terrorised the city and flooded the streets with 'Bolly'. I learned to swan in and out of the Carlton Club as if I owned the place, and to expect gratitude from weary government ministers trying to reconnect to the young. At one party I noticed a man skulking, ignored in the corner. I later discovered he was John Major.

With all the cockiness of youth, naturally I found most of the proverbial rich and famous dead boring and they certainly didn't impress me in the least. For me it was all about pushing, pushing to see what I could do, what limits I could reach. The world was exciting and my own personal oyster, and I could do anything I wanted if I put my mind to it.

I'll teach you to write if it kills me, the editor of the women's pages would say through gritted teeth. God help her, it nearly did, poor woman. An honours degree in English from Edinburgh University was ill-suited to the pacy, punchy prose needed for a daily tabloid, and so I sweated and cried my way into this new career. I learned to look at issues in a different way, and learned a cynicism which I did not realise then, would over time attack the roots of the bubbly enthusiasm which attracted people to reading what I wrote.

I soon found business people far more interesting than actors and celebs and moved on from showbusiness and women's pages to the financial pages. I liked the chutzpah displayed by people who worked with millions. And then I reached my limit.

At 2pm on my first day on the Business section, I was standing in the ladies' loo in the Black Lubyanka, having a panic attack; I had to write 800 words on traded options by 4.55pm and I did not know the first thing about them. The door opened and the late great columnist Jean Rook swept in, immaculate as ever, to find me in full meltdown. She wasted no time mixing cold water on my face with this good advice.

'Never underestimate the advantage of total ignorance and the power of the silly question.'

Good advice I have since used in every area of my life – including on my allotment. For example, er, which way up do you plant a potato? No shame in asking. You could argue that the composition of a potato is every bit as miraculous as a traded option – and both have been known to make people go hungry when they fail.

* * *

Time, alas, is one commodity which cannot be traded. So in Scotland, there is an urgency about autumn, an unmistakable apprehension. Here it is very hard to buy Keats' lines about mellow mists because, trust me, there is absolutely nothing mellow about a Scotch mist in autumn. It eats into your very bones. Winter stands in the wings waiting. This apprehension is even mixed with a small measure of fear, which is very hard to explain or justify in any logical manner in this centrally-heated world, but it is best to label it. Fear of what the winter will bring, fear of the cold, fear of how we shall cope. Sometimes I even feel like Corporal Jones running round shouting 'Don't panic!' Yet fear of winter is like fear of death, both are a waste of time and have to be fought and kept in line.

Actually, to be fair and less dramatic, autumn in Edinburgh starts rather well. It comes disguised, a Trojan horse clip-clopping into town pretending to be summer during the Edinburgh Festival. Everyone is deceived for days, which is all rather jolly. Then suddenly, without warning, winds with that particular icy bite race down the Royal Mile, unbalancing the colourful street performers, who are working the crowds. We may be dressed for summer, but the winds nip and tell a different story. T-shirted tourists look up at the sky perplexed as if for clues, but we natives know what's happening. It's arrived. Time to show a bit of character, not flesh. We wouldn't dream of sitting in Princes Street Gardens without a thick cardie and an umbrella in our bag. We rediscover vests. Vests. I remember Ella's shock on seeing Madonna on the TV news, walking down the red carpet at the Oscars with the prerequisite décolleté. 'But Mummy she's not wearing a vest!' Hold the front page! Evidence, if any were needed, that in spite of being a nice girl from St Albans, I have begotten a true Scot.

Slugging it Out

I hate slugs. Both the human and the animal variety.
The barefaced way they operate, obstructing progress and
consuming my hard work! They have no shame and no
conscience. As a financial journalist with an allotment,
I periodically do battle with both. As I did one Friday last
month, when I pinned down some shifty slugs in stripy
shirts, working for a certain amoral multinational for whom
the term corporate social responsibility is PR speak for
we-don't-actually-give-a-flying-toss, only to arrive at the
allotment that evening to find their cohorts in the animal
kingdom finishing off my lettuces. Boy, do I love a fight!
By Monday both varieties had been squished. It is instructive
to see how panicked, post-Enron multinationals become
when fund-managers and pension fund trustees are targeted
in discussion on their less than ethical practices, while on
my allotment, their animal colleagues – clearly corporate
slimeballs in a previous life – became history, thanks to
gallons of instant coffee, the latest scientific revenge exciting
gardeners everywhere. Don't tell me polluting exploitative
multinationals create wealth and slugs are vital for digesting
vegetable matter – they're still slugs!

It doesn't take many weeks' weeding to realise that an
allotment is not just a plot for growing
vegetables, but a parallel moral universe.
Here, as the couch grass, mares' tails and
snails do their worst, it's a battle of good
against evil, beauty against ugliness,
strength against weakness. So, my (still
sceptical) colleagues observe, people go

slightly barking on allotments, then? Probably! But what better way of staying sane! Don't they know stress-related illnesses are costing the NHS – ie. taxpayers – £11 billion a year?

Now forget weeds, and let us start thinking about strange exotic creatures from outer space. Men. For if Men are from Mars and Women from Venus, you can see which planet an allotment holder is from, at 50 paces. Martians you see, must be in control. Gallons of high chemical weed killer and other instruments of world domination are poured over the ground, vegetables drilled into submission in rows like conscripts. Insubordination invites instant attack with a hoe. Compost heaps are not piles of rotting teabags, but weapons for mass cultivation fenced in with manly planks; bonfires are executed with mathematical efficiency. Picture our annual Flower and Veg Show, not a fun afternoon admiring each other's marrows, but the horticultural equivalent of the medieval joust. Exhibitionists fight to the death. Size matters. Women of course don't get it. The Martians look over the fence at our efforts and shrug. They have to do this a lot, because more women are taking on plots than men.

Women you see, do it for fun. Time off for bad behaviour please! Allotment gardening is the New Sex, giving a whole new meaning to the phrase Green Pass. We spend quite as much time drinking, reading magazines and chatting to our neighbours as we ever do with a hoe. We're in Heaven. We LIKE clumps of foxgloves and forget-me-nots in around potatoes and rose bushes in the carrot patch. Not for us feudal male pecking orders of allotment committees, for we take the high moral ground. Our male colleagues may be keen contributors to the profits of the chemicals sector, but we're Organic Baebes, the key man in our lives, a 19th-century Quaker called Henry Doubleday, whose Research

Association is an online must-visit (www.hdra.org).
In between thinning our onions, we pore over his catalogues,
and fantasise about Calypso strawberries and pale blue
Twongas, the latest in autumn squashes. It's a national,
unheralded camaraderie. Are you into HDRA? Not 'alf.

Berry Good not to Sweat the Small Stuff

Just back from holiday? Had a great time and now feel like
death warmed up? According to a recent Adnams Brewery
Internet survey, most people find that their post-holiday
glow disappears in just 24 hours, replaced by a vertical
plunge into gloom and stress, which centres on the seemingly
overwhelming pile-up of irritations in home and office life.
Somehow, when in the grip of these back-to-work blues,
all the nice things about returning home – seeing friends,
catching up on gossip, being back in your own home and
more to the point, your own bed – somehow doesn't add up
to a row of beans. So you may imagine the slough of despond
I experienced post-holiday on being greeted by an allotment
that, having been left in a reasonably tidy and productive
state just a fortnight before, now resembled an unloved
jungle ruin.

It's that half-empty glass syndrome. Somehow my pleasure
at my waving six-foot high stalks of sweetcorn was out-
weighed by the weeds nearby, now grown more or less to
the same height. Did it rain every day while I was away?
Foolishly, I allowed weeds to obscure the joy of finding
bushes groaning with fat juicy blueberries, raspberries large
enough to be passed off as tayberries, and the first sweet
brambles. I enjoyed meeting up again with my fellow
plotholders and swapping excess produce, yet inside I was

seething at how nettles had buried my strawberries, rhubarb and beans.

I rather think the post-holiday blues come because we do too much too quickly after a holiday in order to reassert control, and also because we fail to plan our re-entry into normal life. So we cannot wait until the washing machine is running seven loads a day, nor do we pause an instant before plunging into that e-mail slagheap, as if it is the marker for our very existence.

So let us become our own expensive management consultants for a moment, and brainstorm for some positive solutions. Perhaps we must start by blurring the line more creatively between holidays and work. Pre-planning could include setting up coloured e-mails to help prioritise replies, or pre-paying for a two-hour appointment at the beautician for our return. Looking back, my late father had the right idea: whenever he could afford it, he always had a week's holiday for himself, pre-booked to begin the day after his return from the annual family holiday, to get over the exhaustion.

In the same vein, this year I am throwing a 'bring your own hoe' Pimm's party at the allotment for all friends who would like to celebrate the holidays by helping me get back to normal.

We Should Stop Buying and Start Growing

Seasons. A word with so many connotations. The society 'season' is over, but new-season clothes have hit the shops, and spring/summer 2006 fashion shows are splashed all over the newspapers. I gather retro military chic is hot, in keeping with our sorry sabre-rattling times, but I am practised in viewing a new season's fashion as a leading economic indicator: short skirts and pastel shades mean good times are round the corner. Long hemlines and dark colours – man the lifeboats.

Of course, down on the allotment, where, let's face it, my own personal haute couture has reached new lows, seasons are the very cornerstone of existence. Now we are in the season of mists and mellow fruitlessness, as most crops are being picked, bottled, jammed and jellied. At dusk, smoke from scores of bonfires wafts across the site. Plotholders suddenly appear ghostly out of the smoke, carrying strings of onions or buckets of tatties. I learned to recognise allotmenteers' special sheepish grin, which is a mixture of unmistakable pride and, in my own case, humble astonishment. This grin says, 'Look what I've done. This lot doesn't come from supermarkets and it will taste of something.' We are the proverbial little people triumphing against the system. Supermarket food may be flown thousands of miles for year-round customer satisfaction, cheating us of the seasons, but now when I go down the fruit and veg aisles, I feel a smug joy, not needing to fill my trolley because I have the food at home, waiting to be eaten.

Allotmenteering is particularly empowering for women, because, over time, it can radically change our ingrained cultural conditioning to shopping. The self-affirmation of growing good food is in another league entirely from the temporary feel-good thrill of retail therapy. Recently, a double-page spread in an upmarket tabloid featured a gaggle of young women boasting that they spend up to £40,000 a year on designer handbags. Perhaps I ought to write a follow-up piece taking this freakish group onto my plot, and showing them how much fun and self-esteem they could gain from howking their own tatties, or plaiting strings of their own onions.

Of course, shopping till we drop for the new season's must-haves generates useful economic activity, employment, advertising revenue plus lots of financial servicing, but in this season of taking stock, let us take time out to celebrate a different harvest.

Walk on the Wild Side

I am writing this column sitting on my allotment, for once completely free of guilt. Yes, my Protestant Work Ethic has been shoved way down into the compost bin along with this week's teabags, eggshells and junk mail, and I am here, notebook in hand, feet propped up on the table, trying to ignore the crows who are mocking me up in the trees. Cor Cor! 'Get a life!' I shout! Cor Cor! Once that was a sign of male admiration but somehow I don't think my old clothes and grungy sun hat is a turn on for anyone. That's the trouble with the Good Life. On a bad hair day you become your own scarecrow.

Still, I am mistress of all I survey. The 60 by 30 feet of it before me anyway. Fifteen months on from taking on this wild overgrown nightmare of a plot, I now have blackberries, plums, pears, blueberries, greengages, kiwi fruit, potatoes, onions, garlic, rhubarb, parsley, gooseberries, parsnips, broad beans, figs and lollo rosso all growing nicely. Of course, I have had a few disasters. Carrots and mange tout flatly refusing to do the business, and after all that copy I lavished on squashes, the wee rotters went down pronto at the first slug. But no matter. This is work in progress.

My new kiwi and fig tree are my latest walk on the wild side. 'Figs and kiwis in this climate!' Hardened gardeners look at me as if I am barking, but this is the stuff of dreams. Just imagine, next year I could try elderberries, mulberries, a walnut tree, even a vine!

My fellow allotmenteers shake their heads and mutter about people climbing over the fence to pick the fruit. They are probably right, but it not just about fruit and who eats it, it is the permanence of trees that matters to me. They are there every day. Good company. I haven't quite got to the point to talking to them, but you never know.

I have long suspected I have the wrong attitude to be a true allotmenteer. For now I am well acquainted with my neighbours, I have learned that behind the apparent patchwork muddle of the allotments, lies a ruthless obsessional drive for perfection, on target to peak just in time for the City Allotments Show. At night, sheds flicker with the lights of those who may stay the night fearing sabotage. Then there is the whispered disinformation. Positively New Labour in its subtleties of spin. 'Old John, he's lost it you know,' I am told. 'Poor old soul... Jimmy? I think he's dead. Look at the state of those brassicas.'

What is it about men needing to win? At the end of last year's Allotment Show antlers locked as my husband (who hates gardening) and the President of our Plot bid against each other for the top prize-winning potatoes which would yield the breeding stock for the next year's champions. Up and up went the bidding. Crowds gathered. Hushed whispers went around the tent as these two alpha males refused to yield. History was in the making. No one had ever seen anything like it. What unbearable tension. Finally the gavel fell. Done! Sold to... my husband. Four potatoes for £10.50.

That's male psychology for you. Naturally, as the admiring

little woman of the victorious male, I stuck them under the
sink and let them chit... until one winter's night when the new
vicar came round for supper. I thought he had said he had two
children and there behind himself, his wife and two toothsome
cuties, were two huge and ravenous looking teenagers.
Shepherd's Pie was the main course. All my neighbours were
out and the shops had closed for the weekend. Er, you guessed.

There are some secrets in a marriage best kept chitting in the
cupboard!

Sobering Lessons of Hurricane Katrina

Outside, all is fog and rain. On days like this when I cannot
go to my allotment, I get my fix online. For out in cyber-
space, a vast community of allotmenteers are telling stories
as rich and varied as the soil they tend. Check out
www.allotments-uk.com/allotments_sites.asp if you ever
feel this country has gone to the dogs for here we can visit
the Bournemouth East Allotments or Nottingham's Shared
Garden. Plots as they fight off the ever-more pressing
attentions of the property developers. What tales of triumph,
disaster and bloody-minded ingenuity!

The medium may be new, but what comes across strongly
is that allotment life is living civic wealth, nurtured and
protected for decades, even centuries, by our forefathers.
So if today's communities fail to protect and support
allotments – and so many are currently under threat in many
major UK cities – this failure is on our watch. Once the land
is gone, generations after us will never know the joy we have
experienced, and that lost wealth becomes common poverty,
however much the properties which occupy the land are
worth to private individuals.

After 20 years of an unbridled market economy it is now increasingly clear that poverty comes in many forms, apart from lack of money. Looking at the terrible TV footage of New Orleans, it is striking is that although no one could have stopped Hurricane Katrina, the real human disaster came through the hollowing out of civic infrastructure for greed by the Baby Boomer generation. So the spending on strengthening the levees – levees built by previous generations for the common good – was drastically curtailed, and the water came in on their watch. And the gap between rich and poor has widened so unsustainably that civic order broke down. However much the Bush administration may see its crowning glory in abolishing inheritance tax, it is civic infrastructure which creates value and lasting wealth, not money. Mountains of money, monuments to human ego, are invariably lost in time; through depressive spending, market fluctuations, revolution, crime, divorces, dysfunctional living and generational decline.

Common wealth is more precious than money, and needs eternal vigilance, for all our sakes. Closer to home, Edinburgh's largest allotment, which lies on a fertile flood plain on the Water of Leith, is soon to be skirted by a new multi-million pound flood prevention scheme. This is where the vigilance will come in. For when future floods are prevented, how much more vulnerable will this precious land be?

OCTOBER

The Crime and the Passion

They say it is enough to make you weep. But that is too pat, and when it happened to me last month, strangely I didn't weep a drop. Not then anyway. I couldn't even summon energy for rage; an interesting phenomenon. I hope it hasn't happened to you, but if it has, you will know what I mean. For it takes a while for the emotions to process criminal vandalism.

So as I walked up to my allotment that Sunday morning four weeks ago, first of all I just took in the blue wooden allotment gate. It had been torn from its hinges, and was now lying wanton and twisted over a blackcurrant bush, squashing the juicy berries. Then I noticed the broken glass. Talon-like shards of it impaling my daughter's toy scarecrow... because of a large log, hurled through her shed window. Then in my very own slow motion silent movie, my eye became a camera panning round... the ripped up bean canes... the broken fence... the damaged mange tout plants I had spent so many hours willing into life. Close up. Thank God they had left my kiwi fruit and fig tree alone. And then my own shed: lock ripped off... radio nicked.

Gripped now by a businesslike cool, I rang the police on my mobile. Bless them, they really did try to sound interested. But as the PC's tone implied, it is only an allotment. Only an allotment. Only then did the pain start eating.

Now you might find all this hard to believe. But you see, to an allotment holder, an allotment is not 'just' anything. Over hours and hours of hard work and loving care, an allotment plot becomes more than land and fresh food, it becomes one of life's most intimate places, perhaps the truest expression of our inner self. A moment in time even, when we are at our freest and most happy, perhaps in a return to a tomboy childhood, because we can muck about and play and get covered in mud.

...But to be practical for a moment. Best tip to anyone in this situation: get an incident number. And if anything is stolen get a separate criminal incident number as well. And if your fellow allotmenteers have been 'done over' too, make sure they report it, but insist they get a separate incident number. Don't let the police lump you all in together as one allotment with one incident number. Why? Well, why should they, when we are all individual taxpayers who have sustained separate property damage? And also because points win prizes in modern policing, or if not prizes, then resources. The more incidents reported in a specific area, the better the chance of a patrol.

And so my dear retired neighbours, who always give my daughter Ella curly kale, had their new shed windows crashed through, while the allotment president lost 17 green-house windows. 'It is almost as if,' the nice police constable observed when I rang, 'they like the crash of glass.'

Quite.

On this occasion I arrived back home muddy and in shock, to find vegan friends standing on the doorstep for Sunday lunch. All I wanted in the world was a large brandy and bed, but zombie style I cooked cauliflower tofu and kept telling myself to get a sense of proportion.

The next weekend the vandals returned. Not so bad this time perhaps, just broken fencing and damaged crops, but it unlocked a sort of cumulative emotional reaction, and so it felt even worse. I couldn't help feeling huge grief. Would there be any end to it? Were they going to come back every week? Could I stand it? Nearby older neighbours, with tears streaming down their faces, agreed that perhaps now it was time to give up – the mental wear and tear was too great. And these, remember, were 'only' allotments.

Coming back that Sunday to scrub the mud and muck off my clothes, face and hair, this time I was due at a smart lunch party at the house of a Green Party member of the Scottish Parliament. What could be done, I asked him over the profiteroles, to put a higher price on allotments? Such was my conviction, by the end he was talking about a beefed Allotment Private Member's Bill attracting cross party support.

Then on Monday morning, when I should have been writing and earning a crust, the anger I should have felt days before suddenly blew in like a force ten gale over North Utsera. Twenty-four hurricane force e-mails went right up to the top of the council and the police. To cut a long story short, we now have a security fence on the way. Regular patrols soon meant the police picked up the vandal gang, who had graduated from allotments to ripping up local gardens. And as for passion in politics, there might even be a new Scottish Parliament Allotments Bill one day soon too. If you are reading this in Scotland, please email your MSP and ask for their support!

So evil did unlock good. Plotholders start talking to each other as never before. And before long they were swapping tales, tips, plants and life stories. The social capital, the non-financial wealth of our allotments is now so much greater than before – something vandals could not have foreseen when they enjoyed the crash of breaking glass.

Hands off, Mr Darcy

I find myself thinking about my allotment at the oddest times. Take last Friday night at the cinema, watching the film version of *Pride and Prejudice*. While disappointed female members of the audience noisily debated whether Bingley or Darcy was the more camp, my allotment flashed into my mind, all straggly leaves and drooping brambles.

Perhaps it is because this vivid new production brings the realities of land up close and personal. Well-endowed livestock wander throughout, and mud is ubiquitous, whether on petticoats or underfoot. I realised how divorced we are from land and earth in our daily lives. How often friends – townies admittedly – tell me that I am the only person they know who gets muddy on a regular basis. This film interested me, because last summer we enjoyed a holiday on the Kent/Sussex borders, during the filming of scenes at the Bennets' house. After the day's shoot, Keira Knightley would tip up at the local pub with the crew, while my two kids, a hardy pair, would go swimming in the Bennets' lake with the swans and the mud.

Recently, the Royal Horticultural Society reported that despite the fact that in the UK we shell out £5.2 billion on our gardens, fewer people these days are 'willing to get their hands dirty, and spend time out in all weathers'. The RHS warns this could lead to shortages of professional gardeners. Have we all become so land-phobic, that we can only enjoy the earth in pre-planted tubs or artfully served up on film?

If land is really no longer part of our mental landscape, then what mugs we are. By 'we', I mean the 99.9 per cent of us living on less than eight per cent of the UK land mass who are brainwashed into thinking bricks and mortar are a source of power instead of land. The 0.01 per cent who own 70 per cent of the land would never buy that. One thinks of Prince William, now gamely doing 'work' experience at Chatsworth (Darcy's Pemberley in the new film) to learn land management in order to enjoy his father's energetic acquisitions.

In Jane Austen's book, Darcy's £10,000 a year comes from land. The novel's core theme, financial insecurity, concerns the Bennets' estate which is entailed away, for lack of male heirs, to the odious Mr Collins. Let's consider our position today. Why is it we ordinary people can't put our houses and, more importantly, the land beneath, into trust for our heirs to enjoy? Why do we continue to accept rules which only favour the Devonshires, Windsors and Darcys? If land and how it is carved up remains to this day the real bottom line, then perhaps it is finally time for the middle class to get their hands dirty?

An End of Season Report

This is the time of year when many people are making new beginnings: new evening classes, new schools, new jobs. I have just packed my son off for his first term at university. How hard that is. But allotmenteers see this time of year as an ending. As nights close in, it seems there is only the long slide into winter to look forward to.

Perhaps now is the time for an end of year report. The great news is that we can be really constructive, with none of the barbed sarcasm which peppered our school reports. You'll know the sort of thing. 'If Swinson worked in life as much as she talked in class, she would do better.' Or, 'Antonia's best will never be good enough, however hard she tries.' Or what about this beauty my extremely bright and charming son once received, 'I hope you have influence, because it is unlikely he'll ever get a job in the open market.' He was nine at the time. (Perhaps readers could advise whether these mercifully rare teachers take modules in mental cruelty at training college, or do they just go power crazed on the job?)

But there's none of that when you are writing your own appraisal. So please find below Antonia Swinson's End of Year Allotment Report:

'After a faltering start due to frost and too much social life, Antonia worked hard this year. She has made particular progress in slaughtering slugs, and worked consistently to keep down the weeds.'

Fruit: Antonia must be congratulated on a healthy crop of blueberries, but she may have to accept that her kiwi is more ornamental than nutritious. Gooseberries were first class this year: heavy cropping and large berries. However, thinking that a greengage tree could be pollinated by another pear tree ten yards away showed lack of homework.

Sweetcorn and tomatoes: outstanding, considering they were grown in Scotland. These should be planted in greater quantities next year.

Beans, peppers and aubergines: must try harder. They were eaten by insects or failed to flower despite polytunnels.

Marrows and courgettes: excellent growth. Well managed, and protected from frost.

New planting: Antonia has proven her perennial optimism by planting a vine – Glory of Boskoop. She has also worked hard to establish 24 herb species.

Allotment Show silver cups: nil (Over-competitive husband taken off to the Outer Hebrides.)

Summary: good overall, though Antonia needs to pay more attention (and money) to compost this winter, and improve her pruning skills. However, this year she has made solid progress and enjoyed herself. Well done.

LAST WORD

IT WILL PROBABLY BE an April day, depending when the letter arrives from the council. They'll go down the path, and perhaps won't be able to stop themselves smiling at the extraordinary individuality of all the plots on either side – the tidy, the teeming, the hopelessly messy and the eccentric. Then they'll come to the end of the path and will stop to open the gate.

They will probably just stand there for a moment, looking. They'll take in the fruit bushes and the small trees and the shrubs and the box beds and the trellis at the back groaning with unkempt brambles. Then they'll walk round the path, maybe pulling a face at the crazy paving and then will open up the two sheds, the big one and the little one. Inside they'll see walls painted in bright colours and painted flowers on the doors. There may be dried and now decaying bunches of lavender hanging down from a hook on the ceiling. They might smile with pleasure all this or else they will frown and say, well this lot's got to go!

Afterwards, they'll walk round the plot, taking in the strawberries and rhubarb – straggly in the spring, and smile disbelievingly at the fig tree and the kiwi. But already their minds will be on what they plan to plant, how they will stamp their own authority on the ground and making it their own, obliterating whoever was here before.

But just for a moment, will they think about the person who was here before, what he, or they will have probably guessed by now, what she looked like, what newspaper she read, what she did for a living, what plans she made, what sort of car she drove or how much she loved this allotment? Will they wonder just what happened to the child who so obviously colonised the smaller shed, and what she did with her life? And will they ever suspect what joy and fun seeped into the soil over the years along with rain, seeds and mulch?

It doesn't matter if they don't, but if they did give it a moment's thought, they might feel even richer.

*   *   *

When I was 18, we moved out of our family home, the only house I had ever known. When the removal men had finished, and we were on the point of shutting the door and handing over the keys, I ran back upstairs to my room and poked a letter in a plastic bag through a small hole in the skirting board tucked underneath the wash hand basin. The letter was dated and contained a description of what my life had been like living in the house. I thought of it as a time capsule, which, when discovered in the future, would be an interesting record of a young girl's life in the latter half of the 20th century. Time has moved on, but when I revisit my home town and walk past the house, a bit of me is still there.

So what will be my time capsule at the allotment? Will it be the fruit bushes and trees now too fruitful to be dug up, the brambles so entrenched it would need an army to lift them, the box beds too useful to be destroyed? Did I make a difference? That's the question most of us will ask at some point in our lives. And I would suggest the question is linked at some level to all our ideas surrounding the issue of possession and ownership. For what, in the end, do we ever really own?

Land and houses, careers, children and furniture: if we are lucky they are leased to us for a season. If we are even luckier, they make us happy throughout that season. But we cannot expect any more than that. In the end, they all go. Ownership is an inaccurate concept. Even the greediest land-grabbing Norman conqueror or grasping family tyrant has to hand over their property to someone else in the end; even the home lived in for a lifetime is nothing to do with you the week after you move out; even the child who is the cornerstone of your existence will be off and away one day, at the glittering career reduced to payslips and press cuttings.

Allotments at least have an honest balance sheet, for we know our lease only lasts as long as we pay our few quid to the Council Parks Department. They teach us that the only asset we do really own, is what we do with the time we are allotted, while our season lasts. That's it. That's the bottom line. We are what we grow, and we can be as rich as we feel.

Useful Websites

Allotments 4 All
www.allotments4all.co.uk

Allotments UK
www.allotments-uk.com

Allsop
www.allsop.com

Antonia Swinson
www.antoniaswinson.co.uk

Ayr Flower Show
www.ayrflowershow.org

British Potato Council
www.potato.org.uk

Charities Aid Foundation
www.allaboutgiving.org

Four Winds Inspiration Centre
www.four-winds.fsbusiness.co.uk

Harrod Horticultural
www.harrodhorticultural.com

Heritage Bulb Club
www.heritagebulbs.com

KidsGardening
www.kidsgardening.com

National Society of Allotment and Leisure Gardeners
www.nsalg.org.uk

National Vegetable Society
www.nvsuk.org.uk

New Consumer
www.newconsumer.org

Organic Gardening Catalogue
www.organiccatalogue.com

Scottish Allotments and Gardens Society
www.sags.org.uk

Soil Association
www.soilassociation.org

South Central Farmers
www.southcentralfarmers.com

The Scotsman
www.scotsman.com

Thompson & Morgan
www.thompson-morgan.com

Thrive
www.thrive.org.uk

Scotch on the Rocks: the true story behind Whisky Galore

Arthur Swinson

ISBN 1 905222 09 2 PBK £7.99

With a new introduction by Antonia Swinson and a foreword by Compton Mackenzie

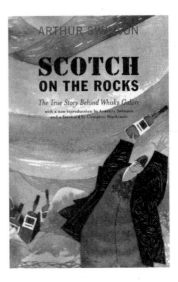

...this story happened to the right people and at the right time. In a chaotic world, this does not happen often; and when it does, it should be recorded.

ARTHUR SWINSON

On the night of 4 February 1941, the SS *Politician* founders off the coast of South Uist. The salvage – nearly a quarter of a million bottles of duty-free whisky and hard currency worth, today, ninety million pounds.

And to islanders across the Hebrides, it's theirs for the taking, hiding, drinking or selling.

This is the true story behind Sir Compton Mackenzie's *Whisky Galore*. Arthur Swinson's careful research casts an honest light on the events leading up to – and following – this tremendous bounty. Awash with contraband, the communities nearby faced unexpected problems: from the government; the police; customs inspectors; and, not least, each other.

'...faced with these extraordinary circumstances, the rash became rasher, the drunken more drunken, the avaricious more avaricious, the convivial more convivial, the generous more generous, the treacherous more treacherous, the selfish more selfish and the commercial more commercial.'

www.scotchontherocks.net

Luath Press Limited
committed to publishing well written books worth reading

LUATH PRESS takes its name from Robert Burns, whose little collie Luath (*Gael.*, swift or nimble) tripped up Jean Armour at a wedding and gave him the chance to speak to the woman who was to be his wife and the abiding love of his life. Burns called one of *The Twa Dogs* Luath after Cuchullin's hunting dog in Ossian's *Fingal*. Luath Press was established in 1981 in the heart of Burns country, and is now based a few steps up the road from Burns' first lodgings on Edinburgh's Royal Mile.

Luath offers you distinctive writing with a hint of unexpected pleasures.

Most bookshops in the UK, the US, Canada, Australia, New Zealand and parts of Europe either carry our books in stock or can order them for you. To order direct from us, please send a £sterling cheque, postal order, international money order or your credit card details (number, address of cardholder and expiry date) to us at the address below. Please add post and packing as follows: UK – £1.00 per delivery address; overseas surface mail – £2.50 per delivery address; overseas airmail – £3.50 for the first book to each delivery address, plus £1.00 for each additional book by airmail to the same address. If your order is a gift, we will happily enclose your card or message at no extra charge.

Luath Press Limited
543/2 Castlehill
The Royal Mile
Edinburgh EH1 2ND
Scotland
Telephone: 0131 225 4326 (24 hours)
Fax: 0131 225 4324
Email: sales@luath.co.uk
Website: www.luath.co.uk